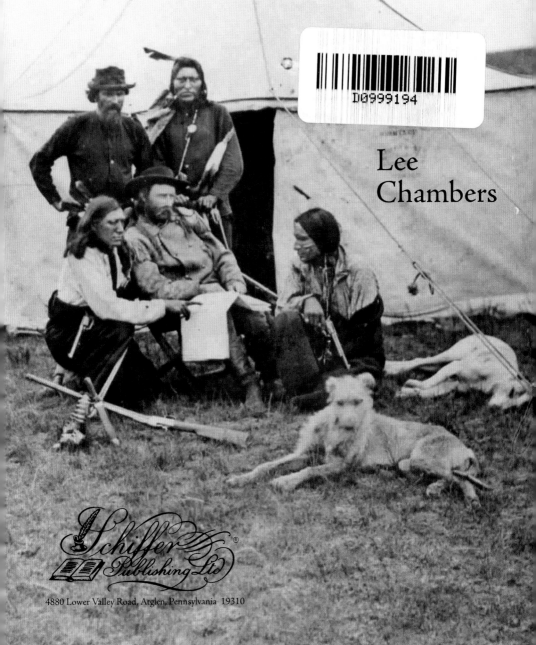

Fort Abraham Lincoln
Dakota
Territory

D0999194

Lee
Chambers

Schiffer Publishing Ltd

4880 Lower Valley Road, Atglen, Pennsylvania 19310

Copyright © 2008 by Lee Chambers
Library of Congress Control Number: 2008925239

Designed by Stephanie Daugherty
Type set in Adobe Jensen/Souvenir Lt Bt
ISBN: 978-0-7643-3026-1

Printed in China

Published by Schiffer Publishing Ltd.
4880 Lower Valley Road
Atglen, PA 19310
Phone:, 610 593-1777; Fax:, 610 593-2002
E-mail: Info@schifferbooks.com

For the largest selection of fine reference books on this and related subjects, please visit our web site at:
www.schifferbooks.com

We are always looking for people to write books on new and related subjects. If you have an idea for a book please contact us at the above address.

This book may be purchased from the publisher. Include $3.95 for shipping. Please try your bookstore first. You may write for a free catalog.

In Europe, Schiffer books are distributed by:

Bushwood Books
6 Marksbury Ave.
Kew Gardens
Surrey TW9 4JF England
Phone: 44, 0 20 8392-8585
Fax: 44, 0 20 8392-9876
E-mail: info@bushwoodbooks.co.uk
Website: www.bushwoodbooks.co.uk

Free postage in the U.K., Europe; air mail at cost.

Dedication

Merle A. Chambers (Mac)
U. S. Cavalry
June 19, 1911 – August 14, 1960

I dedicate this book to my father, Cavalry Sergeant Merle A. Chambers, and to his mount, Goldie.

Action took place in the Philippines during World War II, where my father had the honor of being in the last active cavalry unit that went into battle astride a horse for the United States, although they were later assigned to dismounted duty.

During the battle at the Little Bighorn on Reno Hill in 1876, several troopers volunteered to get water for the thirsty soldiers. They carried canteens, pans, kettles, and anything that would hold water. This action earned these men the Medal of Honor.

Some sixty years later my father and his troops were pinned down by Japanese rifle fire during the Battle of Leyte Gulf. My father volunteered to carry as many canteens as he could to obtain water for his troops. He crawled to the nearest water hole and, while lying on his stomach filling canteens, received two wounds from a sniper, but he was still able to return to his troops with the water they so direly needed. Though gallant and brave, Sgt. Chambers did not receive the Medal of Honor for this action.

Times and criteria change for the disbursement of medals, especially the Medal of Honor. Sgt. Chambers did not perform that challenge for a medal, he did it because his men needed water. For me, my father will always be a hero in the United States Cavalry.

TSGT Merle A. Chambers (U.S. Cavalry) on Goldie. c.1942, *Courtesy Rick Chambers*

In Memoriam

#2 *Courtesy Edith Wright*

SSGT Virgil L. Wright, U.S.M.C.
April 15, 1949 – May 02, 2005

In memory of my lifelong friend.
Always in my mind,
forever in my thoughts,
and buddies for eternity.
No one could have wanted a truer friend.

Semper Fidelis

Acknowledgements

When an author acknowledges those who have assisted them, I often wondered how they seeded them in importance. Is moral support more important than the person who spent hours editing the manuscript? Is the person who researched material more important than the individual who offered the use of equipment? Is someone who gave the author time to write uninterrupted more important than the financial support? Is someone who found a needed photo more important than those who listened to me talk about my book constantly, thus giving me moral support?

These questions have made the Acknowledgements Page the *most difficult* to compose. I have divided my thanks into sections to help alleviate this dilemma. I offer my heart felt thanks to everyone who assisted me. This book could not have come to fruition without *all* of you!

I must point out two people in particular for their help on this book. The first person has always been there throughout my life. He is not only my brother, but also my best friend. Thanks, Rick, for all that you have done for me. "Watch your top knot."

The second person has put innumerable hours and assistance into the finalization of this book. He is my dear friend and I thank you, whole-heartedly, Barry Martin.

Wisconsin and Florida: Rick Chambers, Merle Chambers, Marjorie Van Acker, Michel Van Acker

Canada: Laura Heydon, Bonnie Heydon, Barry Martin, Corrine Heydon, Lorraine Thiebault

Michigan: Ann Saviniemi, Colonel Phil Poole, U.S. Army, Judge Advocate General, Retired, Robert Zimmie, Lt. Colonel John Birberick, U.S. Army, 177th Military Police Brigade, Retired, Master Sergeant Kieth Birberick, U.S. Air Force, Dave Ingall, Monroe County Museum, Elvi Saviniemi, Rafael Saviniemi

46th District Court: Donna Beaudet, Iris Bowman, Keith Chin, Rachel DeCoster, Laverne George, Joe Goodrid, Wendel Gramlich, Captain Rene Hinojosa, U.S. Army, Autumn Kennedy, Frank Kohl, Marie Konicov, Sally Price, Brian Smith, John Stevens, Serah Wiedenhofer

North Dakota: Jeff Hoffer, Fort Abraham Lincoln State Park, Dan Schelske, Fort Abraham Lincoln State Park, Lucy Dahner, Fort Abraham Lincoln State Park, Dan Kautzman, Fort Abraham Lincoln State Park, Jim Davis, State Historical Society of North Dakota, Sharon Silengo, State Historical Society of North Dakota

Illinois: Quentin Castricone, Jodie Creen Wesemann, Rock Island Arsenal Museum, Jennifer Malone, Rock Island Arsenal Museum

Pennsylvania: Tina Skinner, Schiffer Publishing Ltd.

North Carolina: Sandy Barnard, author and friend

New Hampshire: Edith Wright, Virgil Wright

Teachers: Mrs. Coopman, 5th Grade, John Deere Elementary, Mrs. Johnson, 6th Grade, Ridgewood Elementary, Mr. Anderson, 7th Grade, Glenview Jr. High, Mr. Diedrickson, 8th Grade, Glenview Jr. High, Mr. Bassier, 9th Grade, United

Township High School, Mrs. Lauritzen, 10th Grade, Township High School, Mrs. Nielib, 11th Grade, United Township High School, Mrs. Glen, 12 Grade Typing, United Township High School, Mr. Francis, 12 Grade, United Township High School, who was the most influential teacher in my life. This book makes up for all the book reports I failed to write for your class. A very special thanks to him for understanding me. Mr. Hanson, Black Hawk College, who taught me to be the best police officer I could become.

And also: John Doerner, Custer Battlefield, Dave Ingall, Monroe County Museum, Sandy Barnard, Al Frasca, Hal Jespersen, Don Wiles, Steven Sclaroff, Rodney Ploessl, Dave Corbin, Don Radcliff, Wendell Gramlich, Scott Kuchta, Mary Ann Fellner-Rapp, Lisa Hale, Kim Monroe, Barry Lubman

Contents

Introduction

For Abraham Lincoln was historically important but it is a little-known fort near Mandan, North Dakota. During the mid-1870s, it was commanded by Lieutenant Colonel, Brevet Major General George Armstrong Custer. Researching Fort Lincoln began as a fact-finding mission on a project for the Fort Lincoln Historical Society that grew into what seemed like researching a living being. It was more than just a fort; it was a soldier's duty station, a protective base for citizens and railroad workers, a life-style as well as a home for those who resided there. Information flowed from history books, historians, local citizens, maps, and, of course, the historical societies and museums. With continued research it became apparent just how important this fort was, other than the obvious point of being commanded by General Custer. It was a keystone in the development of the United States. This fort teemed with soldiers who were intelligent and abounded with military skills. It housed numerous former generals of the American Civil War as well as future generals who learned their trade as they progressed through the ranks with promotions on the western frontier.

A fort is built for two reasons: as a base of operations for a military force and for the safety of troops, should an enemy attack. Fort Lincoln is no different. It was built for military forces to protect the crews constructing the Northern Pacific Railroad across the Dakota Territories from Indian attack, and to house the soldiers needed for this operation.

Because Fort Lincoln's existence was solely due to Indian tribes, its history must begin with an explanation of the area as it was before the fort was built. The first known inhabitation of the Mandan/Bismarck area occurred sometime around 400 B.C. to 400 A.D. Not much is known about them, since this was prehistoric times. On top of the hill where the Infantry Post was located is a mound of earth constructed by the Indians. The only known inhabitants of the area were the Hopewell Indians, also called the Mound Builders, around 200 B.C. to 700 A.D. The Hopewell Indians resided mostly in what is now Ohio, but had traded for goods that came from the west coast, Canada, the east coast, and the south. The mounds make us believe they were Hopewell Indians. Other Indians existed throughout North America but only the Hopewell built mounds in this time period. Mounds were built for a variety of purposes: spiritual, burial, animal shapes for whatever purpose, and for housing. The Hopewell Indians inhabited the lands only as far north as Northern Illinois and Eastern Oklahoma during their height of influence, but with their vast avenues of trade some of their influence may have drifted northward into the Mandan/Bismarck area with small satellite groups. Later, the Mississippian influence of mound builders, 700 B.C. to 1500 A.D., would encompass the Mandan/Bismarck area, but that would be well beyond the date estimation of the mound at Fort Lincoln. Like the Mandan tribes who inhabited this area some 1,300 years later, the Hopewells were agricultural, growing crops of beans, corn and squash. The reason for the demise of this culture is completely unknown.

Besides the mound builders, the Mandan/Bismarck area supported several other Indian tribes over the years. The Arikara Indians migrated from the Texas area. The name means "horn," referring to the knob of hair on their forehead. They were a sedentary culture that preferred to grow crops, then supplement them with hunting. Their housing consisted of earth lodges. The Assniboin Indians migrated from Northeast Wisconsin and Canada. They were a nomadic culture that hunted for their food. Their housing was the tepee. The Cheyenne Indians migrated from Minnesota and Indiana, but they were forced out by the Chippewa, then made to move further south by the Mandan and the Hidatsa. Their Cheyenne name means, "people of different speech." They were a semi-nomadic culture that did some farming along with hunting and their housing was wigwams. The Chippewa Indians (Ojibwa, Anishinabe) migrated from the Wisconsin, Michigan, and Ontario region. Their name comes from the puckered seam on their moccasins. They were a semi-nomadic tribe that preferred to hunt and fish and their housing was wigwams. The Hidatsa Indians migrated from northeast Wisconsin. A sedentary culture, they farmed with some hunting, and lived in earth lodges. The Mandan Indians migrated from the Ohio area. Their name means "those who live along the bank of water." A sedentary culture, they farmed, with some hunting and their housing was earth lodges. The Sioux Indians (Dakota, Lakota, Nakota, Santee) migrated from the Wisconsin area. Their name means "snake in the grass." They were a nomadic culture, they preferred to hunt for food, and their housing was tepees.

Wrong or right is not the purpose of this book. It has been said many times that the Indians did not own the land. That is a misconception. Indians not only owned the land but they fought to the death to retain it or to obtain more. They did not own it in the sense we understand today, but owned it for the survival of the tribes. Land meant one thing only, survival, and survival involved food. Whether it was meat, plants, or water, they fought to control land that contained hundreds of thousands of acres of food and water for sustenance. An example is the Sioux, who initially lived in Eastern Wisconsin but were driven out by the Chippewa into what is now North Dakota and Montana. This was not a friendly, mutual decision; it was all out war. Another point of land ownership is not an easily accepted pill to swallow, but it is fact. Both sides were trying to get the best deal concerning the land. The white man knew the value of land in their society and also knew the Indians would accept what was considered paltry sums of money and trading goods for prime land. The Indians society, on the other hand, thought they were getting the best of the deal because they did not believe anyone could own the land personally. Thus, by receiving the trading goods for their land they thought they would accept the goods and still be able to retain the land as well, thus besting the white men in the trade. The Indians understood fighting for land to survive, but not ceding land forever for trade of goods. Land was everything to both sides, but neither understood the value placed on it by the other's culture or how tenaciously each would fight to take control or retain vital land.

Fort Lincoln is rich in history involving Indians. With the convergence of rivers in the Mandan/Bismarck area, it was a natural trading site for various tribes. This area was instrumental in the development of the United States and involved probably two of the most well known explorers for the United States, Meriwether Lewis and William Clark, and probably the most famous female explorer in United States history, Sacajawea .

During Lewis and Clark's winter stay near the site of where Fort Lincoln would be constructed seventy years later, they became acquainted with a Shoshone girl whose Indian name meant "Bird Woman." She was the daughter of the Shoshone Chief and had been captured by the Hidatsa tribe. Her destiny in American history became etched in stone upon her marriage to a French Canadian trapper/guide by the name of Trousseau Charbonneau, who won her while gambling. Lewis and Clark needed a guide to help them go up the Missouri River, and hired Charbonneau for the 1803 "Corps of Discovery." That was the exploration of the Louisiana Purchase territory that the United States bought from France. By hiring the Frenchman, it was understood that his wife would also accompany the expedition, not only because she was his wife but also because they would be traveling through her homeland, which was ruled by the Shoshone and that made her a great asset. This quirk of fate made this teenage girl the most renowned female explorer in the United States. Not only would her name become synonymous with Lewis and Clark, but her son, born during the exploration, would have a stone pillar in Montana named after him and future generations would visit it. The pillar is called "Pompey's Pillar" and the teenage girl, guiding one of America's most prestigious explorations, was Sacajawea.

In the following pages, you will be introduced to Fort Lincoln, originally commissioned as Fort Mc Keen, and learn its purpose, construction, armament, and battle tactics. The story will provide you with an idea of how it may have been without modern conveniences. The story is about the fort, from its inception in the 1870s to its abandonment in the 1890s and its rebirth in the 1980s. It is a wonderful historical trip to one of the most significant forts in our history. Enjoy it as you read and view the photographs and illustrations, but most of all enjoy your escape back to the 1800s.

Chapter 1
Life at Fort Abraham Lincoln

#3 1873 Fort Lincoln Cavalry Post. *Courtesy Little Big Horn Battlefield.*

When the average person is asked to picture a 19th century fort, more than likely his or her mind's eye envisions one similar to Fort Apache in Arizona. These prototypical forts had four fenced walls of de-limbed trees spiked at the top with a blockhouse on each corner sitting high atop the fencing (palisades) for a better view and easier defense. Inside the fort are various buildings made of neatly cut and equally sized logs, with cannon at the ready. Access in and out of the fort was gained by two huge gates that swung wide, so that wagons and mounted troopers could easily pass through them. Not so with Fort Abraham Lincoln.

Fort Abraham Lincoln is not as well known as some of the 19th Century forts, such as Fort Apache, Fort Dodge, Fort Sumter or Fort Leavenworth. However, Fort Lincoln became one of the largest and most important forts for the development of our nation. It was more like a city than the prototypical fort. The actual confines of the fort, if they can be called that, stretched over one mile from north to south and over one-half mile from east to west. The fort was huge for this time, in light of the fact that the fort was susceptible to Indian attacks until the late 1880s. Situated along the west banks of the Heart and Missouri Rivers approximately five miles south of Mandan, North

#4 1874 Behind Officer Row. *Courtesy Little Big Horn Battlefield*

#5 1875 Fort Lincoln hillside view. *Courtesy State Historical Society of North Dakota,C0743*

#6 1876 Fort A. Lincoln. *Courtesy Little Big Horn Battlefield.*

#7 1876 Fort Lincoln winter scene. *Courtesy Little Big Horn Battlefield*

#8 1882 South view. *Courtesy State Historical Society of North Dakota, D0514*

#9 1885 View across river. *Courtesy State Historical Society of North Dakota, C1830*

#10 1891 Southeast view. *Courtesy Little Big Horn Battlefield.*

#11 Fort Lincoln. *Courtesy Little Big Horn Battlefield.*

Dakota, the fort spreads out in a serene setting that is hard to visualize as an arena of sporadic combat. Libby Custer, General Custer's wife, reported watching a battle take place between the fort's Arikara Indian Scouts and a Sioux war party, while she was in the comfort of her house.

Fort Lincoln would become part of the Army's Division of the Missouri. This division encompassed 15 modern states, covering over one million square miles, 99 various Indian tribes containing 192,000 Indians who the Army had to protect, provision and supervise. The division consisted of 76 forts and camps, 8 regiments of cavalry, 17 regiments of infantry staffed with 17,819 soldiers.[1]

The Division Headquarters was located in Chicago, Illinois, with General Sheridan commanding four separate departments. The Department of the Dakota covered present day North Dakota, South Dakota, Montana and Minnesota with its Headquarters located in St. Paul, Minnesota. The Department of the Platte covered present day Nebraska, Utah, Wyoming and Iowa with its Headquarters located in Omaha, Nebraska. The Department of the Missouri covered present day Missouri, Kansas,

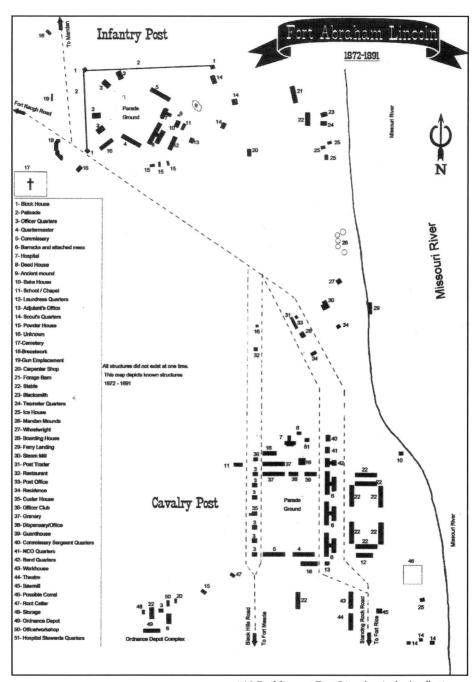

#12 Buildings at Fort Lincoln. *Author's collection*

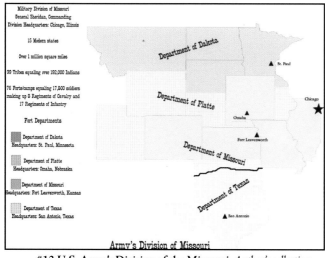

#13 U.S. Army's Division of the Missouri. *Author's collection.*

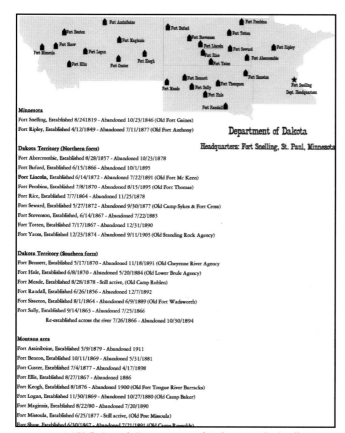

#14 U.S. Army's Department of Dakota. *Author's collection*

New Mexico, Colorado, Illinois, the northern part of Oklahoma and the northern part of Texas with its Headquarters located in Leavenworth, Kansas. The Department of Texas covered present day southern part of Texas and the southern part of Oklahoma with its Headquarters located in San Antonio, Texas.

The closest forts to Fort Lincoln were Fort Rice (28 miles), Fort Stevenson (72 miles), Fort Seward (112 miles), Fort Totten (128 miles), Fort Pembina (130 miles), and Fort Snelling, the Department of Dakota Headquarters, (408 miles). The distances between forts created special problems when one was attacked and in need of assistance. If a fort did not have a telegraph line, a messenger on horseback was sent to the nearest fort and returned with reinforcements. The response time depended on whether the closest fort was a cavalry post or an infantry post, which could not respond as quickly. This was one of the reasons Fort Lincoln was reassigned as a cavalry post.

The fort began as an infantry fort named Fort Mc Keen, but within five months those plans had to be altered to serve as a dual-purpose fort, billeting both infantry and cavalry personnel. Prior to this change, the infantry was performing tasks as best they could, but they were lacking in pursuit abilities once the Indians attacked and fled. The infantry was out-maneuvered with hit-and-run tactics by mounted Indians. The soldiers were unused to this type of combat and they had difficulty adjusting. They were more accustomed with walls of soldiers facing one another shooting it out. To offer better protection for the railroad crews, a mounted military force was direly needed to pursue and capture attacking warriors. Realizing the fort was out-dated logistically in its protection capabilities, it was quickly updated to include cavalry troops.

Once the decision was made in 1872 to add the cavalry post, it was also decided to change the name from Fort Mc Keen to Fort Abraham Lincoln. The renaming of forts was not an unusual practice. The "powers that be" could change a fort's name to honor a friend or someone they admired. Some forts have had three or four names adopted before a final name was chosen. The most important decision was who would occupy Fort Lincoln. No better force could have been assigned than the flamboyant, successful Indian fighters of the 7th Cavalry, commanded by the Civil War Hero, Lt. Colonel (Brevet Major General) George Armstrong Custer.

To understand General Custer, you must read about his Civil War exploits. Only then can one understand why he attacked as he did at the Little Bighorn and at Washita, Oklahoma. He always accomplished what he was trained and ordered to do, so well in fact that the table on which the Conditions of Surrender of General Robert E. Lee's army was signed was given to Libby Custer by General Sheridan, stating, "I know of no person more instrumental in bringing about the surrender than your most gallant husband."[2]

One must also recall the time period, the 1870s. War tactics, morals, and accepted norms were vastly different in Custer's time. Then it was an accepted tactic to attack the enemy's home base to destroy food, weapons, supplies and even future generations of warriors. Appalling and sad as it is, this type of attrition was acknowledged as a good battle plan. We have become familiar with the excuse, "I was only following orders." In fact,

#15 General Custer. *Courtesy State Historical Society of North Dakota, C478*

Custer was following documented orders from his Superior, General Sheridan, the second highest-ranking officer in the Army. His orders were to "Attack villages, food supplies and families, kill or drive them from lodges, destroy ponies, food, supplies, and shelters, then hound them."[3] If women and children were killed, it was regrettable, but justified, since it resolved the war more quickly. This order became known as the "Winter Campaign" or is referred to as a "Total War Campaign" designed to destroy Indian resistance by depleting their self-sufficiency. During the summer months, Indians were mobile with plenty of food, water, and warm weather. By attacking Indians in the winter months, when they were sedentary, Indians could not replenish their food supplies, hunt buffalo for skins to make more tepees, replenish pony herds, or obtain the supplies needed for more weapons. The reasoning was that it made the Indians more dependent upon the U.S. Government for food and shelter, which in a morbid and ironic twist protected the Indians from more decimating mortal battles.

Custer may have been many things, good and bad, but it is without doubt that he was a brave man and a leader. During his Civil War battles he led cavalry charges, even though he was a Major General. An eye-witness account of General Custer attacking Confederate forces at Gettysburg states, "Custer leaned forward in his saddle and yelled, 'Come on you Wolverines!' Then Custer, with total disregard for his own safety, gripped the reins in his teeth and grasped his revolver in his right hand and saber in his left, while spurring his trusty mount four lengths out ahead of his regiment and charging into enemy masses."[4] Can you imagine today having a one-star or two-star general running in front of his men attacking a fortified position? It is surely a tactic of the past.

Flags

The battle flag was important because it was a visual aid to the soldiers during combat. It offered a focal point so that they knew the location of their unit. They also knew their commanding officer would be near the flag so if he was needed they could find him. The battle flag also served as a rallying point should they become separated from the rest of the troops.

The flags were also very important for morale since they were from home states, counties or even cities. Some of them were handmade, probably by sweethearts, wives or sisters. If not made by the women, more than likely they raised the money to purchase the flags to send their men off to war. It gave the soldiers a mental tie back home. They were proud of their origins and would fight tenaciously to prevent dishonor to the flag. But should it be lost, destroyed or captured, it was a disgrace and morale would plummet. In some instances the troops would lose the will to continue fighting. Even today legal battles continue being fought as southern states try to retrieve the lost battle flags from northern state's museums.

It was more than just a flag to follow. There were color guards ("colors" being a name for the flags) to protect the flag bearer as well as the flag itself from capture and to make sure the flag was always readily seen. The flag bearer was usually a sergeant or promoted to a sergeant. Should the flag bearer become incapacitated for some reason one of the color guards would drop his rifle, pick up the faltering flagstaff, raise it above his head and continue the charge. It was considered an honor to carry the flag and only the bravest and best were given this distinction. The color guard was not allowed to lower their weapons to fire at the enemy. The precious ammunition, usually single shot rifles, must be saved to protect the flag should an attempt be made to take it. Casualties were always highest near the colors, thus giving an idea of the importance of the flags and the Color Guards. The infantry had six to nine color guards for two flags but the cavalry had only one flag bearer followed by one corporal.

Battle flags were also very important to the general staff during combat as well. The flag, as long as it was flying, would show the commanding officers where their companies were located. This aided the general staff in the deployment of troops as well as in the locating of company officers so that further orders could be sent to the company commanders more readily. The staff could also tell by the lack of the flag if companies had fallen, surrendered or were captured. There was a difference between cavalry flags and infantry flags. Of course we see the guidon shaped flags used by the cavalry but the main difference was size. The regimental flag carried by both services were drastically different. The cavalry regimental flag was 2 feet 3 inches by 2 feet 5 inches, which was over 5 square feet of material. But the infantry regimental flag had over 40 square feet of material! The regimental flags were usually all blue with an eagle in the center and the name of the regiment on a banner under the eagle.

#16 U.S. Cavalry Guidon. *Author's collection. Courtesy Fort Lincoln Commissary Store.*

This type of national flag was carried by the cavalry. It was smaller than the type carried by the infantry and it had the "swallow tail" design used for cavalry company flags.

This was General Custer's personal headquarters flag. It was the same shape and size of regular company guidons. It was 3 feet tall by 5 ½ feet wide. Though technically only a Lt. Colonel who should not have had a personal flag, he had full rights to his own flag due to his Brevet Major General rank. Besides the red and white Company Guidon, this flag may well be the most recognized Cavalry flag known. Something of interest about this flag is that it was handmade by Libby Custer for her husband, General Custer, in 1865. It was recently sold at an auction for $896,250!

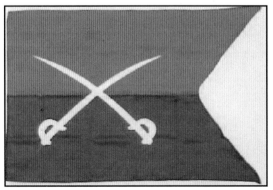

#17 Custer's Headquarters flag that was hade made by Libby Custer. *Courtesy, theflagguys.com*

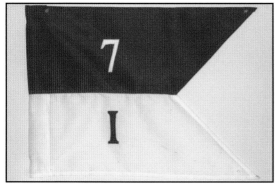

#18 7th Cavalry Company I Guidon. *Author's collection. Courtesy Fort Lincoln Commissary Store.*

This flag was a company guidon. Red on top and white on the bottom, the white number designated the regiment and the red letter designated the Company.

Horses

General Custer went one step further with company recognition. He opted to color-coordinate the troopers' horses.

Company A	=	Dark Bays (brown)
Company B	=	Light Bays
Company C	=	Sorrels (reddish brown)
Company D	=	Blacks
Company E	=	Grays
Company F	=	Light Bays
Company G	=	Mixed colors
Company H	=	Light Bays
Company I	=	Light Bays
Company K	=	Sorrels
Company L	=	Light Bays
Company M	=	Light Bays

Band members, non-commissioned officers (Sergeants and Corporals) and trumpeters rode Grays.[5]

Many people may have taken this colorization of companies incorrectly. Granted, it would look great for parades, but it was also used for troop recognition during battle. It would be much easier to distinguish an entire company of horses of the same color in the gun smoke, swirling dust and the smoke from fires than a small company guidon that may or may not be there. Initially the troopers disliked the order colorizing the company's horses because most generally a horse and rider were assigned specifically to each other for the duration of an enlistment. Empathy can be given to both sides. The troopers and horses were familiar with one another, building up a common trust. It was more than handler and animal, it was a team being split up. In the long run easy recognition of forces could make the difference between life and death. In reflection, for the 7th, the long run didn't matter. Did Custer assign horse colors to companies for showmanship or did he do it because he was being an innovative commander? Maybe it was a smattering of both.

Custer at one time with his newly formed command made his men practice shooting twice a week, both mounted and dismounted, with many winning awards for their expertise. He had 40 of his best shots made into an elite force under the command of his Adjutant, Lieutenant Cooke. For their skills they did not have to do guard or picket duty. These shooting exercises were when most forts did not practise firearms for years on end, if ever. Custer was concerned about the trooper's abilities with firearms, as well as their equestrian skills. It was said the 7th could be recognized from a distance due to all the parade drills Custer demanded.

Buildings

Each fort's location designated the building materials used in its construction. Some forts were built of stone or even adobe, which is sun-dried mud with maybe some prairie grass mixed in for added strength. Whatever their make-up they were ever changing due to fire, renovation, added construction or deterioration.

Fort Lincoln was built upon land with trees readily available. The buildings at the fort varied, some were log, most were framed, some were built with what they could find and some even had canvas roofs. One thing most of Fort Lincoln's buildings had in common was that they were all mostly built off the ground. This may have caused them to be colder in the winter by allowing the wind to whip below them but it saved the floors and base supports from rotting and having to be replaced or repaired. At least 100 buildings had been constructed at Fort Lincoln over the years.

The following list is of the buildings at the fort. It had 2 Adjutant's Offices, 1 Boarding House, 1 Band Quarters, 5 Barracks, 3 Block Houses, 1 Black Smith Shop, 2 Bake Houses, At least 1 Carriage Shed, 1 Commanding Officer's Quarters, 2 Commissaries,1 Commissary Sergeant's Quarters, 2 Carpenter Shops, 2 Dead Houses, 1 Forage Barn, 1 Ferry Landing, 2 Granaries, 1 Guard House, At least 1 Gun Shed, 2 Hospitals, 4 Ice Houses, 2 Laundress' Quarters, 1 N.C.O. Quarters, 11 Officer Quarters, 1 Office/ dispensary, 1 Office/ workshop, 1 Officer's Club, At least 50 privies, 1 Post Trader, 1 Post Office, 4 Powder Houses, 1 Photographer Shop, 2 Private Residences, 2 Quartermaster Store Houses, 1 Restaurant, 1 Root Cellar, 11 Stables, At least 6 Scout's Quarters, 1 School House Chapel, 1 School House/ Chapel, 2 Saw Mills, 2 known Store Houses, 1 Teamster Quarters, 1 Theatre, 6 unknown buildings, 1 Wheel Wright, 1 Workshop, and an unknown amount of wood sheds.

Location and Water

The cavalry post was built upon a relatively flat area along the Missouri River about one-half mile south of the infantry post. The Missouri was a treacherous river, though it could be serene in places. Over time, as with any fast moving water, the land in and around the river changes. In some areas it could change weekly. A resident of the fort reports hearing huge sections of embankment plummeting into the river with a roar due to erosion. The erosion was such a problem for riverboats the Army protected on the Missouri, that riverboat captains had to be able to "read" the Missouri River, because it was never the same by the time it came to their return trip. This is of course before the taming of the river with levees and dams. The Missouri River for the troopers was life as well as death. It gave sustenance of water needed for survival of humans as well as crops and animals. It gave ice for cooling drinks in the summer, use by the hospital, maintaining summer supplies of fresh meat or maybe a stolen visit to one of the four ice houses to escape the paltering heat. But it also took life in the form of drownings, evident by the grave markers in the post cemetery.

The cavalry post was placed on the flats near the Missouri River, south of the infantry post that was built upon a hill 300 feet above the Missouri River. The problem for the cavalry being located on Mc Keen Hill was plain and simple…water. The water had to be drawn from the Missouri River in barrels then delivered throughout the posts. Due to a sudden 300-foot elevation of the land above the river, there were no wells at the infantry post. With the advent of 600 horses going to the fort, the supplying of water would be a major task. Each horse would require about ten gallons of water per day. That totals 6,000 gallons of water a day just for the horses. That gallon usage would require over 13 wagons each day being hauled up the highly inclined slope. Then there was the additional water needed for cooking, cleaning and drinking as well as supplying water for the infantry and cavalry quartermaster's horses and mules.

It required six mules to pull the water wagon. This is not excessive when you realize the weight of the water and the steep incline to Mc Keen Hill. If the water were delivered by barrels, the weight alone is staggering. Water weighs eight pounds per gallon thus one 59 gallon barrel of water weighs 472 pounds, the barrel weighed an additional 98 pounds. If each wagon could hold three barrels, it made the load over 1,700 pounds. The wagon weighed 1,800 pounds so just one wagonload of water weighed over 1 ¼ tons that had to be hauled up a 9% grade. In addition to hauling all this water there were the wagons of grain, hay and forage that would have to be laboriously pulled up the hill. It would have been an around the clock ordeal moving wagons back and forth for water and feed instead of walking the horses to the river.

The Missouri River is not a clear river at all. The best description of the water is the color of weak chocolate milk or coffee with cream in it. Muddy is the most often used term to describe it. A good analogy was, in order to drink Missouri River water one put the water in one's mouth, sucked it through one's teeth and what went through the teeth was swallowed but what stuck to the teeth was spit out onto the ground. Even by leaving the water sitting in a glass for a time most of the sediment would sink to the bottom but it would still remain murky. A couple common practices to help settle the sediment was to add a teaspoon of alum or place a piece of bread in the glass. The alum helped but then the side effect was the unwanted flavor of the alum. Try putting a teaspoon of baking powder or alum into a glass of water to experience the taste.

Diet

The diet at Fort Lincoln seemed bleak, at best. It may have been better than most forts but worse than others. Depending on where the information is obtained, the fare varied. Three soldiers described their daily meals as follows:

	Soldier 1	*Soldier 2*	*Soldier 3*
Breakfast:	Coffee Bread Hash	Coffee Bread	Coffee Bread Hominy Hash
Noon Meal:	Coffee Sliced Beef Bread	Coffee Boiled Beef/bacon Bread Bean or rice soup	Coffee Bread/Hardtack Beef/Buffalo Peas/Potatoes
Supper:	Coffee Bread	Coffee Bread	Coffee Bread

A fourth soldier stated the supper menu was the largest meal of the day, yet we see from others that the noon meal seemed to be the largest. Either way, the daily nutritional requirements we have today were totally lacking then.

Their main diet consisted of beans, bacon, hardtack, flour, coffee, bread, salted beef or pork, a smattering of vegetables, if available, assorted desiccated vegetables (dehydrated vegetables pressed into dried cakes often called "desecrated vegetables" or "baled hay"), local fruits when in season as well as buffalo, deer, fish, and game birds. Condiments were salt, brown sugar, vinegar, molasses, and maybe even an occasional bottle of ketchup. Daily rations consisted of: either 12 oz. of pork, bacon or 1 lb. 4 oz. of salted beef or fresh beef. With either 1 lb.6 oz. of soft bread, flour, 1lb. of hard bread (hard tack) or 1lb. 4oz. of cornmeal. For every 100 rations, the soldiers were given the following supplies which would be drawn by the Commissary and then distributed to the mess halls: 15 lbs. peas or beans, 10 lbs. rice or hominy, 10 lbs. coffee, 15 lbs. sugar, 4 quarts of vinegar, 1 lb of adamantine (the hard part of animal fat used in making candles) or 1 lb. of Star candles (actually spelled Stearin, candles that have a prescribed burn rate), 4 lbs. soap, 3 lbs. potatoes, 1 quart of molasses.

Like any post in the military, fresh vegetables were a prize, but in the winter months they were an impossibility to obtain. The commanding officers gave permission for the officers to have their own gardens, as well as the enlisted men having one down by the river. Custer had his own garden behind his quarters in the back corner of the yard with a tall fence surrounding it. The gardens were made to supplement their stark meals and any excess produce was sold off for company needs or desires. If one company's garden abounded with crops while another company's garden was bleak, the prosperous company could sell its excess to the less fortunate company. With the extra funds the company could purchase other produce they did not have enough of or they could purchase items needed for their barracks.

Storing the vegetables was a problem until the officers approved the construction of cisterns for food storage or the root cellar behind Officer Row. Basically a cistern was a hole in the ground with some type of covering, or it was built beneath the building to keep out the freezing weather. Even then, the produce had a limited time before it spoiled. Custer had an actual basement in his house instead of a cistern where he stored food along with his pet cougar. However, there was a problem in getting food stored in the Custer's cellar because Mary, his cook, refused to go downstairs to retrieve the supplies… even if the cougar was a pet!

A few questions always arise about the soldier's food. The most common being, what is hardtack? What is hominy? And what was buffalo meat like? Hardtack, also called "hard bread" resembles a large soda cracker in appearance about four inches square and approximately .125 inch to .250 inch thick with 16, .125 inch holes in the center. It was made of flour and water, thickened to a paste then placed in a press to create its shape and perforate the 16 holes. Once baked, it became very hard and could last for years if kept dry. (Some bakeries may bake the hardtack two and even three times before packaging.) Hardtack was used in various ways: they could have jam, fat, lard, or anything spreadable on it and eat it like bread…that is if they could get their teeth through it. It could also be crunched up by pounding it with a rifle butt or rock and placed in coffee or mixed in with bacon grease, making it a soggy goo called "skillygalee" or "cush." If sugar or berries were available they would be mixed in as well. Another treat was, crushed hardtack mixed with a can of condensed milk to make what they called, "milk toast." The soldiers often complained of the hardtack being moldy or infested with weevils, worms or maggots. The mold developed from either becoming wet after being opened, or the baking company not allowing the hardtack to dry thoroughly before packaging. Hardtack had its aliases such as "teeth-dullers", "sheet iron", "molar breakers", or "worm castles." One soldier's complaint about the bugs being so thick in the hardtack was, "I threw it away three times but it kept walking back."[6] The 19th century soldier often joked about hardtack just as soldiers did 100 years later with C-rations and K-rations, or as we do today about Spam.™

Hominy (also known as grits) is ground, hulled kernels of corn that have been stripped of the bran and germ, the interior part of the grain. The kernels are then ground into the consistency of coarse sand. Actually, the term "grits" also can refer to wheat or oats. But it is the word "hominy" that makes it corn grits. We have probably all had grits, in the true sense of the word, without realizing it but it has been disguised as a malted breakfast cereal: creamed wheat. Mixed with a little milk and sugar, like oatmeal, hominy grits are a palatable meal.

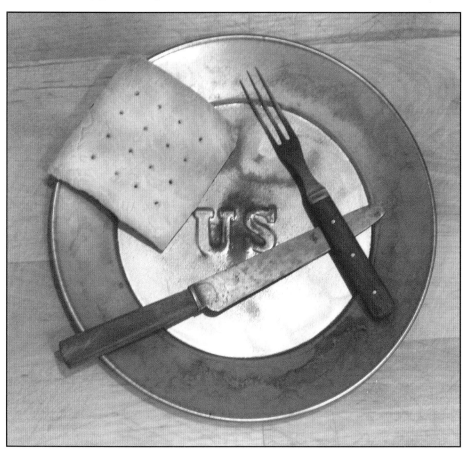

#19 Hardtack. *Author's collection.*

#20 Grits (uncooked and cooked). *Author's collection*

#21 What a soldier's meal may have been. *Author's collection.*

Buffalo meat is not given its true accord. When mentioned that the soldiers had to eat buffalo it is made to sound as if the consumption of buffalo was undesired. However the exact opposite is true. Buffalo meat is leaner than beef, so with less fat it is better for you. The flavor of the meat is very tasty and today it is usually sold in upper scale butcheries, of course it is a more costly cut of meat.

Canned items could be procured from the post trader at exorbitant prices, almost twice the normal price. The post trader was like a small general store but had to be listed as a franchised trader with the government, giving them a monopoly over what the soldiers could buy as well as being able to mark up the prices without concern. Mainly the soldiers would obtain canned fruit, tobacco, canned oysters, cans of condensed milk, pickled pigs feet, canned meat, or whiskey (when approved by the commanding officer) from the trader. Since the soldiers were only paid about every two months or longer, the need for credit was immense. The goods could be charged to their accounts, called "Sutler's checks", with a five-dollar maximum. The stipulations were that the bill was to be paid on the next payday, plus they had to have written approval from their company commander who co-signed the credit payment. During pay call the post trader sat next to the paymaster with his list of soldiers owing him money.[7] If the soldier failed to pay the Post Trader, his direct superior would make life miserable for the delinquent soldier until the bill was paid, since the company commander was responsible for the past due account. The Post Trader surely had the influence to have the superior get his "pound of flesh" until the bill was paid. Another source for goods was to make a trip into town. Prices were cheaper but credit was almost unheard of for the soldiers. The reason being that if a soldier transferred, deserted, was killed or just didn't want to honor his debt, the store owner had no recourse to reclaim the monies due him.

The officers were also offered the luxury of buying cattle, hogs and chickens for their private use. The officers would pool their money to buy the livestock then share the meats upon slaughter. The entire fort personnel would also be given the opportunity to go out hunting and fishing for further supplements to their meagre meals. For hunting birds they would have to provide their own shotguns. It is not impossible to shoot a bird with a rifle or a pistol but the exit wound from a .45 caliber destroys a lot of meat so shotguns were desirable and very expensive, sometimes costing over three months' wages for the common soldier.

Climate

The Mandan/Bismarck area has a mean temperature of 43 degrees Fahrenheit. When referring to mean temperature at Fort Lincoln it can be taken two ways. Between two extremes or just plain mean and nasty weather. The area is known for its cold as well as its heat. Visiting Fort Lincoln in the summer is very nice but it can become unbearably hot. Imagine how uncomfortable it must have been in the hot prairies wearing uniforms made of wool with flannel shirts or worse yet, the ladies wearing layer upon layer of clothing with their dresses dragging in the dirt. Though scratchy, heavy, and bulky the wool uniforms had more than one good quality. In winter, wool is very warm, but should the clothing become wet, it was the only material that helped to retain body heat, thus preventing hypothermia. Other materials when wet actually act as a wick, drawing away body heat.

The area was also noted for its hungry mosquito swarms. Libby Custer describes sitting outside for relief from the indoor heat, because doors and windows had to be closed to keep out the hungry insects. Once outside she was forced to add more clothing such as wearing a head net, gauntlets, raincoat, scarf and either the general's boots or wrapping her legs with newspapers then pulling socks up over the paper. The animals were decimated because they could not stand still long enough to graze and some were driven mad by the incessant attacks from the ravenous pests.[8] However, soldiers fared better than Libby with her friends and family. Chewing tobacco was readily available at Fort Lincoln. The soldiers would chew the tobacco, spit the juices into their hands, and then rub it all over their exposed skin to repel the mosquitos. At first we all wince as we think about the odor and appearance of this home remedy. But we need to recall the washing habits of the soldiers were few and far between, especially out on campaign. Besides everyone had an odor so it was not as noticeable.

On the other hand, the winters can be miserably cold. Libby Custer also told of the time, that as she and the general were traveling on the plains and were forced to hold up in a shack because of an extreme snowstorm. While in this unheated wreck of a building, she was nursing a very ill general while trying to keep the door barricaded to prevent the horses from gaining entry to escape the cold and bitter wind.

The area also has a recurring high wind that never seems to be gone for more than a few days at a time. In the wintertime the wind feels like it is slicing right through you, reducing your core temperature. In the summertime it seems to be cooking you as much as a convection oven would.

Civilian Contracts

Two items contracted out to civilians were the gathering of hay and wood. The hay reaped throughout the area consisted of prairie grass. Piled onto hay wagons that could hold from one to two tons, it was taken to the fort where it was piled into ricks (mounds) hundreds of yards long.[9] Supplemented by grain, the horses were given 14 pounds of hay which would amount to over 8,400 pounds each day for 600 horses. The horses were also fed fodder (forage) as well. Fodder contains a mixture of elements including corn stalks, hay, grass or straw, which is the stalk of wheat after the grain has been taken off. In photo #6, in the right foreground of Cavalry Square, are light, colored objects that may be hay ricks.

The amount of wood needed for heating over 78 buildings and cooking and washing over 700 people must have been tremendous. A cord of wood is four feet wide by four feet high by eight feet long. This does not sound like a lot of wood until you have to fell the trees, de-limb them, cut them up into manageable sizes, haul them to the fort, cut them up to stove lengths and then split them, all of which was done by hand axes and hand saws. In photo #3, the two dark, long shapes to the far left, and above the suspected corral site may be stacks of logs.

In a recent re-enactment, it took twenty-four cords of dried oak wood to heat a restored two-story insulated house built in the 1890s for one year. At Fort Lincoln

#22 Wood wagon. *Courtesy State Historical Society of North Dakota, 0003-130*

they had to heat with cottonwood, a soft wood with only half the heating units (British Thermal Units) of oak. Using those figures they would need over 1,872 cords of wood per year just for heat alone. That would make a row of wood over two miles long. This explains why the area near the fort was deforested, making it appear as though a defoliate had been used. In lieu of wood for the stoves in the barracks and small buildings, buffalo chips (dried buffalo manure) or knotted prairie grass could have been used.

Entertainment

Entertainment at the fort was quite varied. From the list of activities, it seems as if the fort's inhabitants were busy at all times. There were dances at the fort or in town. Once a month the enlisted men had a dance to which officers were invited. There were sleigh rides, picnics, buffalo hunts, wild game hunts, fishing, horse races, foot races between the fastest soldiers, horse shoes, boxing, gambling, card games, concerts, and baseball. There was a rivalry between the Fort Lincoln Activities baseball team and the Fort Rice Athletics. Captain Benteen, when not out on patrols was stationed at Fort

#23 Hay wagon. *Courtesy State Historical Society of North Dakota, 0232-077*

Rice. He was an avid baseball player and it must have given him great pleasure when his team would defeat the Fort Lincoln team, since it represented Custer, whom he detested. There were two billiard tables at the post trader store as well as one loaned to Custer for the Commanding Officer's Quarters upstairs.

But just like today they had their lulls of idleness. The boredom in the winter months especially must have been tiresome. Even in the cold the troops would volunteer for escort duties of the mail, supply wagons or the paymaster.

There were numerous assignments for the troops throughout the month. Besides protecting stage coaches there were scouting parties of various types as well as guarding the monthly supplies being delivered, mail deliveries, bridge building, erecting telegraph poles, general maintenance of the fort buildings, etc. The volunteers for the cutting of ice and winter water collection would be given a ration of whiskey at the beginning of the day and one at the end of the day.[10] These were probably the two most brutal jobs at the fort but the soldiers considered them well worth the discomfort for the approved alcohol allotments.

Then of course there were the unapproved "visits" across the river to the south delta of the island called Whiskey Point, The Point, or Carleton City. This point, by whatever name it was called, had a collection of taverns and houses of ilrepute supposedly off limits to the soldiers, which were almost impossible to regulate. Who could be expected to stop over 600 men from quenching their thirst for alcohol or their lust for women? Alcoholism and venereal disease (called the "French Pox") was prevalent among the soldiers. It was reported at that time that almost 4% of soldiers were alcoholic and 8% had venereal diseases.[10]

The trip across the Missouri river could be made by ferry, but since the visits were clandestine they more than likely took bull boats across. Swimming across was not a real option due to the current being so fierce. Because of the strong current some type of floating device was necessary. A "bull boat" was more a device than a boat. The framework was made of willow branches bent in a huge bowl shape about four feet across at the top and eighteen inches deep. A bull buffalo hide, (thus the bull phrase) was used due to the fact that a bull hide was less likely to leak than a cow buffalo hide. This hide was then stretched around this framework, making the entire craft weigh about 30 pounds. The hair was left on the hide because it prevented the craft from spinning and helped repel the water. Once in the water it was not very steady because it bobbed around like a cork but it served its purpose for short trips. The closest analogy that can be used is that it would be like floating in a huge salad bowl.

Rank and Insignia

The chain of command at Fort Lincoln had two similar yet dissimilar structures; one was infantry the other cavalry. Basically they were the same with regards to manpower, with the exception naturally of the cavalry being responsible for the horses and their accoutrements. The command structure at Fort Lincoln consisted of 12 companies of cavalry and 2 companies of infantry. The Regimental Command of the infantry differed from a Regimental Command of the cavalry in that the infantry was based upon 10 companies and the cavalry was based upon 12 companies. The following Regimental Command numbers are based upon ideally staffed regiments which Fort Lincoln was known *not* to possess.

#24 Bull boat. *Author's collection.*

#25 Bull boat. *Author's collection.*

Infantry Command

Fort Lincoln had two companies of infantry under its command. Each command had 1 Colonel, 1 Lieutenant Colonel, 1 Major, 1 Surgeon, 2 Captains, 2, 1st Lieutenants, 2, 2nd Lieutenants, 2, 1st Sergeants, 10 Sergeants, 16 Corporals, 2 Trumpeters, 156 Soldiers.

Cavalry Command

The 7th Cavalry had 12 companies in its command. Each command had 1 Colonel, 1 Lieutenant Colonel, 3 Majors, 1 Surgeon, 12 Captains, 12, 1st Lieutenants, 12, 2nd Lieutenants, 12, 1st Sergeants, 60 Sergeants, 96 Corporals, 12 Trumpeters, 12 Farriers, 12 Saddlers, 12 Wagoners, 936 Troopers[11]

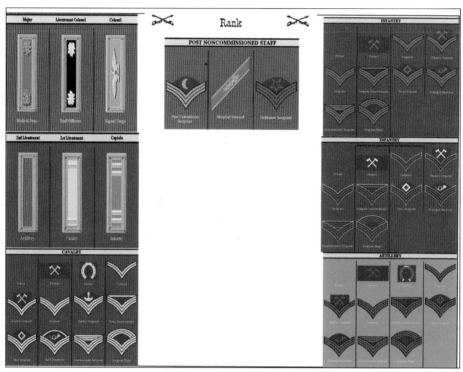

#26 Rank and insignia. *Courtesy Rodney W. D. Ploessl, BA, MSc,*
United States Army Insignia Home Page..

The numbers are deceiving. Sometimes a Colonel was technically in command of a fort but never saw the fort because he was on detached service, such was the case with Custer's Colonels. At the beginning Custer's immediate commander was Colonel Andrew Smith. When Smith retired the colonelship was promised to Custer but was given to Colonel Samuel Sturgis instead. Both Colonels had been given administrative assignments, thus taking them out of the field and in direct command of the 7th Cavalry. These assignments placed Custer as the Field Commander of the 7th, which was more than likely the overall plan. The numbers only show mandated staff size. Not only were the ranks lessened by those sent on detached service, but should a soldier be absent from service due to punishment details or desertion, the voided positions could not be refilled to make up a full compliment. Another misconception for the amount of troopers assigned to a company is that it was assigned the magic number of 78 troopers per company. But due to the attrition rate through desertion, etc. on the frontier it was decided to increase the privates to 100 per company. But during Custer's Command at Fort Lincoln, it was down to 54 troopers per company.

The troopers had various assignments and a uniform spoke volumes to those who understood the color schemes. Colors were not only used to make a uniform look appealing, they told what service the soldier was assigned. Infantry uniforms were blue with either blue or white piping. Cavalry units had yellow piping and artillery units had red piping.

Additionally, the insignia designated where the soldier specialized. A lozenge (diamond shape) on a Sergeant's chevrons indicated he was a 1st Sergeant. A bugle was a trumpeter, while a chef's hat designated a cook. A saddle designated a saddler, and a horse shoe indicated a ferrier/blacksmith. A red cross with emerald green trim and a caduceus (a staff with wings on top with two serpents entwining the staff) designated medical staff.

Uniforms

This is not an attempt to describe an exact uniform worn by the soldiers at Fort Lincoln during the Indian Wars. For that matter could anyone possibly describe the typical uniform worn by *all* soldiers? At that time period, a soldier's uniform out west was basically a melting pot of whatever was available, especially while out on campaign. One soldier's uniform, to use the term loosely, could be part Civil War issue, part recently issued clothing, part civilian wear, or part Indian buckskins, which were shirt and pants made from the skins of the deer. Mistaken as purely ornamental, the fringe on the buckskins played a very important part in functionality. When the buckskin became wet it was very heavy. The fringe on the buckskins would act as a wick drawing the water away from the main garment as the fringe flopped around in the air, thus drying the main garment much quicker.

Uniforms changed periodically over the years due to new designs, needs, style changes, improved materials, or favors and or debts owed by the Quartermaster's Office with uniform manufacturers. However, uniforms out west were mandated by what was available. The Quartermaster Store House may have had an over abundance of Civil War era pants but not the blouses. There could be recently issued uniforms in stock or no uniforms at all until the next shipment arrived, which could be months away. Due to shortages, soldiers would piece together a uniform or repair what they had. Of course the only readily available materials to use for repairs were old canvases used for wagon covers, tarps or tents, and faded out uniform rags that were non-repairable. If military clothing was not available for replacement or the garment was non-repairable, civilian clothing could be used or even buck skins. Sometimes the mismatched uniforms were so hodgepodge that the only way they could distinguish the rank of the soldier was if they personally knew the soldier or officer.

The following articles are just a small variety of uniform clothing that *may* have been worn by soldiers at Fort Lincoln. All styles and models will not be addressed since an entire book could be written on the uniforms between 1872 and 1891.

Drawers

A one-piece garment from the ankles to the neck, the drawers were styled like what we currently call "long johns". They were made of cotton and buttoned up the front from the crotch to the neck. There was a convenient long opening in the back to allow the soldier to use the privy without having to take off his shirt, then unbutton the drawers and pull them down. The cavalry drawers had a three quarter length leg that went to the middle of the calf to facilitate the cavalry style boot.

Socks

Socks were made of cotton or wool and were off-white in color.

Shirts

Shirts were grey wool flannel pullovers with long sleeves and three buttons at the neck opening. Cotton shirts were also permissible as were civilian shirts as long as the striped and checkered patterns were small.

Pants

Pants were sky blue in color with top cut pockets. The 1873 model waistband had a small belt and buckle size adjustment on the back of the band. Pants used by the cavalry were the same style but the seat and inner thigh were double lined to prevent wear and tear while sitting in the saddle. Non-commissioned officers wore a stripe down the outer leg with the appropriate colored trim, depending on the soldier's assignment. A sergeant's stripe was approximately one inch wide and a corporal's stripe was approximately a half inch wide.

Braces (suspenders)

Braces were made of white cotton. The adjustments consisted of piercing prongs that did just what it said. The prong pierced the cotton straps to hold the adjustment. The braces had an "X" or "Y" configuration in the back portion depending upon the soldier's preference.

Vest

The vest was an optional piece of clothing but if worn it must be dark blue.

Shoes and Cavalry Boots

The shoes were black leather brogans which had a four and one half inch high top. They had square toes so they could fit either foot. The soles were either sewn on or attached with small wooden pegs. Brass nails would come later. When a manufacturer with questionable ethics was confronted about the soles falling off after a few weeks of marching, his explanation was that he thought the shoes were for the cavalry. To help prolong the life of the shoe's heel some soldiers would have a "U"-shaped metal cleat nailed upon the heel.

There was actually more than one style of cavalry boot. The one we are most familiar with is the knee high style we see in the movies. They were called "Jeb Stuart" boots or "jack-boots". The front of the boot was approximately 20 inches tall with the rear of the boot having an approximate 17-inch height. The toes were also squared so they could be used on either foot. Once the boots were worn enough they would eventually conform to the shape of the foot. The reason for the tall front of the boot was to protect the soldier's pants and legs while riding in the underbrush.

A second style of cavalry boot was called a half boot. The front of the boot was approximately 12inches tall and the rear of the boot was approximately 10 inches tall. The front of this boot served a secondary purpose. When cleaning the stables the soldier would lift his pant leg above the two-inch lip, thus pulling the rear of the pant leg up also. This lip would hold the pant leg up while the soldier worked, keeping the heel of the pant out of the manure.

Kneckerchief (neckerchief)

Kneckerchiefs were an optional piece of clothing. But a very versatile piece of clothing it was. It could be a triangular piece of cloth or it could be a square piece of cloth doubled over into a triangular shape. The length from point to point was approximately three feet. It was either a solid dark color or even a small-checkered design. No, not yellow! The yellow neckerchief was a Hollywood innovation.

The kneckerchief could be used for a variety of purposes such as a bandage, a sling for an injured arm, a tourniquet, and scarf to cover the face in a dust storm. It could be wetted down and placed around the neck or placed inside the crown of their hat to cool the soldier; it could be a cape to cover the nape of the neck from the sun or as a makeshift hat should their cap be lost, etc, etc.

Blouse (jacket)

The blouse was dark blue with a single row of five buttons. Non-commissioned officers wore their chevrons on the upper sleeve between the shoulder and elbow. Colored trim or cording on the blouse depicted the branch of the service the soldier was assigned.

Hat/caps

The forage cap or kepi style hats were widely used but the favorite seemed to be the fatigue hat. The forage and kepi hat were made from wool. They were flat on the crown with the rear being higher than the front giving it a sloping angle towards the visor. The visor, sweatband and chinstrap were made of leather. The forage hat and the kepi had basically the same design. The main difference between the two hats being, that when the forage hat was turned upside down the crown unfolded, taking the shape of a small cloth bag. The forage cap was designed to, well...forage. One must remember a lot of a soldier's sustenance was obtained from the wild. The forage hat was then used as a bag to gather nuts, berries, etc. It could also be used to feed and water their horses.

The fatigue/slouch hat/campaign hat, whatever it was called, was made of felt with a wide brim all the way around the crown, similar in design to a cowboy hat. The wide brim was designed to keep the sun and rain out of the soldier's eyes and off the nape of their neck. Hats were required to have an insignia on the front to signify the soldier's area of expertise. An example being, a set of hunters horns signified the infantry but was later changed to crossed rifles and crossed sabers signified the cavalry.

Great Coat (over coat)

The great coat was sky blue in color to match the pants. It had double-breasted front with buttons and a cuff-length shoulder cape. Non-commissioned officers wore their chevrons on the lower sleeve between the elbow and wrist with the appropriated colored trim. The colored inner lining of the cape that we see in the movies came after 1873.

Gauntlets (gloves)

Gauntlets were an optional attire. They were made of soft buffed leather that covered the hand, fingers, wrists and forearms.

All of these regulatory pieces of clothing could be literally thrown by the wayside and a "uniform" of makeshift materials used in replacement of the worn out equipage.[12] These substitute uniforms may help give credence to the theory on what possibly happened to General Custer at the Little Big Horn. One Indian's testimony states, he had no idea of who was leading a charge across the river ford into the Indian Village but he was dressed in buckskins. The Indian reports shooting the buckskin clad soldier and as the soldier fell the entire charge halted. The troopers stopped, picked up the fallen leader of the charge and then retreated towards "Last Stand Hill". Two facts are outstanding here, Custer always led his charges and Custer was wearing buckskins at the Little Big Horn!

Even though a soldier wore a uniform it did not necessarily make him a combatant. Certain personnel were only staff related which meant their job assignments were at the fort, so they never left the post for campaigns. This is not to say they didn't pick up a weapon if the fort was attacked. Another specialty, the Ordnance soldier, was assigned to the post. The Ordnance department was responsible for the issuance and storage of all weapons including the ammunition for the weapons. If companys or regiments were transferred the Ordnance soldier remained at the post. Once assigned to a post the Ordnance soldier stayed there until he personally transferred or the ordinance department was transferred.

Once assigned to a troop, a soldier could spend his entire enlistment with that unit. It was expensive and very time consuming to allow soldiers to transfer. This is not to say it wasn't done, it was just a rare occurrence.

Desertion

There was however another way a soldier could "transfer" and that was through desertion, often called a "French Leave." Desertion was commonplace in the 19th century military. The reasons for desertion varied from poor food, poor living conditions, only using the military for food and shelter during the winter months, running off to gold fields, to tyrannical officers or N.C.O.s (Non-Commissioned Officers, such as Sergeants or Corporals). It seems the most common reason was due to treatment by supervisors. Custer may have had one of the highest desertion rates due to his sternness. Some of this treatment was due to Custer wanting his troops to be well trained or well disciplined where they would function without question. However, Custer did fail in this aspect. He did not lead by example when it came to following orders if it didn't benefit him. In fact he was arrested three times for disobeying orders. Ironically the third infraction almost saved his life. He had been placed under arrest for disobeying orders by leaving Washington, D.C. without permission of President Grant. Custer was in Washington giving testimony into the corruption of the post trader system, and almost missed the Little Big Horn Campaign had it not been for General Terry and General Sheridan presenting a case of leniency to President Grant.

You would think once a soldier deserted he would be done with military service. However that was not the case. Many soldiers deserted from one unit for whatever reason, then turned around and enlisted in another unit under an assumed name. There were the cases when the soldier who deserted would accidentally meet up with a soldier who knew him or he would be assigned to aid the unit he deserted, thus being discovered. The punishment for this infraction could vary from being court-martialed and serving time in the guardhouse, expulsion from the military with a dishonourable discharge, or branding on the hip with a D, or satisfying the term of enlistment for both units.

Enlistments

The reasons for enlistments varied; anonymity, excitement, a steady job where all decisions were made for the soldiers, food and housing; running away from families or enemies or law enforcement; or just needing a place to stay until Spring set in. Enlistments were also a foreign affair. During the 19th century, enlistment was 42% foreign-born, with 20% being Irish, 12% German, and the remaining 10% having varied nationalities. At Fort Lincoln the ratio was 32% Irish and 20% German. The Irish were so much in demand as soldiers that one unknown Civil War General stated, "I would prefer Irish soldiers to any other. They have more dash, more élan, are more cheerful, and more enduring than other soldiers. They make the finest soldiers that ever shouldered a musket and never lose their good humor."[13] The military during the mid 1800s was not too much unlike the French Foreign Legion with men from all over the globe - *"the butcher, the baker, the candlestick maker."*[14]

The soldiers came from all phases of life, including former clerks, carpenters, cowboys, miners, politicians or criminals looking for anonymity. Most were Civil War Veterans who wanted to continue their military career where they were provided with food, lodging and most their decisions were made for them. Regardless of ethnic background or station in life, the soldiers were all volunteers who signed on for up to five years; enlisting at a whopping $13.00 per month.

Punishment

Punishment for infractions at the fort varied depending upon the infraction and the officer, or the Sergeant administering the punishment. In modern times civil rights attorneys would be slavering over the inhumanity, but even then there were punishments deemed inhuman.

Miscreants of military protocol or regulations were dealt with in the following manners:

- Carry a 30 pound log on the shoulders for hours;
- Weed the parade ground;
- Weed the gardens;
- Collect and deliver water for the officer's quarters and barracks as well as the bakery two times a day;
- Cut wood for the officers' quarters or the bakeries;
- Ride the wooden horse (The offending soldier was forced to sit astride a fence rail for hours and adding to the humiliation they may be ordered to hold a mock saber at his shoulder);
- Carrying a ball and chain (having a 12-pound ball attached to a chain that was clamped around the ankle, which was often called "Uncle Sam's watch chain");
- Carrying a sign around the post stating the offense, such as being a thief, malingerer, etc;
- Placing the trooper's horse's reins about his neck and then led to water (for soldiers who failed to water their horse);
- Being bucked and gagged (A stick was tied in the soldier's mouth, and then his ankles and wrists were tied with a larger stick that was placed under his knees and over his elbows.);
- Shaving half of one's head and parading around the post while a drummer played "The Rogue's March," then being led off post to be evicted forever. (This is where the term being "drummed out of the service" originated.)

Riding the "Wooden Horse"

#27 Soldier riding the "wooden horse". *Author's collection*

One punishment not condoned by the military was "Running the Gauntlet." (The offending soldier had his shirt removed and then he was led to a double row of soldiers facing each other, creating a narrow path between them. The soldier was then forced to run down the human pathway while the soldiers struck the offender with objects such as belts, saber knots, and reins.)

Daily Schedule

The daily schedule for work details was not consistent between forts. The exact schedule of duties would be dictated by the commanding officer

#28 Soldier being "bucked and gagged".
Author's collection

depending upon available manpower, post location, post needs, and the commanding officer's idiosyncrasies. All duties would be designated with a particular bugle call.

#29 Guard mount. *Courtesy State Historical Society of North Dakota, A4363*

4:30 a.m.	Wake the cooks
5:00	First call - Wake the troops
5:30	Reveille - Roll call
	Guard mount - Inspection
	Guard Detail - Guard selected and marched to posts
	Stable Call - Cavalry troops groom and water horses
	Sick call
	Drill - Infantry marched, Cavalry performed parade drill both mounted and dismounted, teamsters practiced wagon formations, and prisoners performed punishment details
	Breakfast
7:00	Sick call
7:30	Fatigue Duty - Clean grounds, barracks, etc
	Drill
10:00	Water call for the cavalry to water the horses. Also this time was designated for the prisoners to refill the water barrels at the bake house.
12:00 p.m.	Noon meal
1:00	Fatigue Duty
	Drill
	Stable call - Water the horses
	Clean equipment
	Inspection
4:30	Drill
5:00	Water call for the cavalry to water horses. Also this time was designated for prisoners to refill water barrels at the bake house
6:00	Supper
8:30	Tattoo - Secure post and prepare for bed
8:45	To quarters - Prepare for lights out and bed check
9:00	Taps - Stop talking and lights out by the last note

As can be seen, the most often called duty was drill. Drill was performed often so that the soldiers could perform their orders properly, effectively and automatically without thinking. It also taught them teamwork. Drill was performed so often one Private wrote home, "The first thing we do in the morning is drill. Then drill, then drill again. Then drill, drill, a little drill, more drill. Then drill and lastly drill. Between drills, we drill and sometimes stop to eat a little and have roll call."[15]

Bugle Calls

Most forts operated throughout the day and night by bugle calls. There were around 32 calls that the soldier must learn and respond to without thinking. Assumption can only take place when saying that the 3 favorite calls were Mail call, Mess call, and of course Pay Day call. The following are the bugle calls at most forts.

Bugle Call	Job Assignment
Assembly	Raise the flag
Captains call	1430 hours (2:30 p.m.)
Charge	Self-explanatory
Church	1000 hours Sunday (10:00 a.m.)
Drill	Assemble on parade ground
Drill march	Self explanatory
Fatigue	Police the grounds, clean quarters, report to other work
Fire call	Self explanatory
First call	Wake troops, assemble buglers
First Sgts call	Go to Headquarters with duty assignments and roll call report
Full dress	Self explanatory
Issue	Assemble to receive distributions
Mail call	Self explanatory
Mess call	Breakfast, noon meal, supper
Officers call	All officers to Headquarters
Orders	Post the orders of the day
Overcoats	After first call put on coats if needed
Pay day	Self explanatory
Recall	General purpose Retreat Lower the flag
Reveille	Morning roll call
School	Self explanatory
Sick call	Go to dispensary for being sick
Stable	Feed and groom horses
Taps	Stop talking lights out by last note
Tattoo	Secure post and prepare for bed
To arms	Self explanatory, Also known as Boots and saddles for the Cavalry
To quarters	Prepare for lights out & bed check
To the color	After retreat, lower the flag
Water	Water horses or replenish water supplies

To hear all the bugle calls, visit: 7thuscav.homestead.com/bugle_calls.html

The Waning Years

Many buildings were added as the fort progressed through the years. But the days came when repairs weren't made; buildings became unwanted or were no longer needed. Some were lost to fire or were dismantled because they were no longer used. Eventually, every building would be gone with most of them being demolished or destroyed in one day when a hoard of scavenging citizens razed the decommissioned fort, leaving only three buildings standing. Some of the farmhouses near Fort Abraham Lincoln had been built from wood either scavenged or stolen from the fort buildings.

#30 "Custer House" being razed. *Courtesy Little Big Horn Battlefield.*

A rebirth had been granted to Fort Lincoln in the 1980s. With the interest of history and a lifestyle no longer understood, a resurrection has begun. We may never have every building rebuilt or even more than one type of building rebuilt such as all four barracks but at least the future can meet the past for a few hours.

Chapter 2

Infantry Post Structures

#31 Infantry Post, 1872 (Fort McKeen).
Courtesy State Historical Society of North Dakota, 00200-6x8-585

The fort began as Fort Mc Keen on June 14, 1872. Its purpose was for the protection of crews working on the construction of the Northern Pacific Railroad through Dakota Territory. It was named in honour of Colonel H. Boyd Mc Keen, who was killed during the Civil War while leading a charge of his 81st Pennsylvania Volunteers at Cold Harbor, on June 3, 1864.

The first Commander of Fort Mc Keen was Lt. Colonel Dan Huston, Jr., who, with approximately 130 men of Company B and Company C of the 6th Infantry, constructed the initial buildings at the fort.[16] After construction, contingents of the 6th and 17th Infantry occupied the fort. Fort Mc Keen had three blockhouses spread out with only two palisades (fences) between them. This palisade structure was surely more psychological than practical with this design. It was felt these two walls were sufficient to protect the more easily accessible terrain, which was very steep to the south and east of the fort without trees or underbrush for concealment. If the solders would have been outflanked at the palisades, the fort was entirely open to attack. The soldiers constructed a bomb proof/cistern below their barracks in order to fight from a fortified position should they be outflanked. (Sgt. Ryan, a former Sergeant of the 7th Cavalry, describes

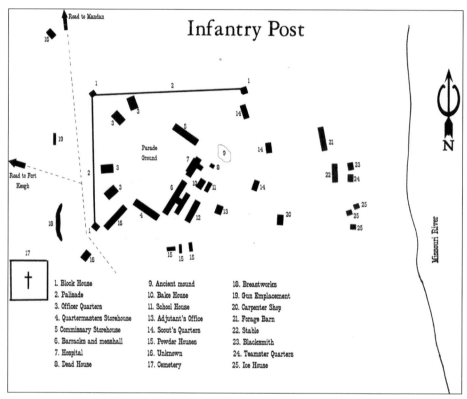

#32 Infantry Post Buildings. *Author's collection.*

these cisterns in his manuscript as well as the bomb proofs at other forts or stagecoach stations.)[17] He mentions other soldiers copying his construction of these pits as well. The cistern/bomb proof at Fort Mc Keen is a beautiful piece of work. It is round (less likely to cave-in or collapse) and the walls are made from fieldstone for reinforcement. It is impossible to tell how deep the cistern is due to the hole being partially filled in over the years with dirt. But the stone walls look just as good as they did over 130 years ago, even being exposed to the elements for 13 decades.

Local cottonwood was used for construction of the buildings and, because the wood was not permitted to "season" (dry out), it created massive warping. It is very soft wood but readily available in the area. The rest of the construction was of inferior materials, with labor coming from the soldiers stationed there who were not professional carpenters, thus standards and building finesse was lacking. As can be seen by the Fort Mc Keen layout or photographs, the infantry post consisted of 3 blockhouses, 4 Officers quarters, commissary, quartermaster storehouse, enlisted men's barracks with attached mess hall, adjutants office, 3 scout's quarters constructed of log, carpenter shop, hospital, dead house (morgue), schoolhouse, bake house, 3 powder houses, a laundress quarters constructed of log, cemetery, breastworks, gun emplacement, and a few unidentified buildings. Other buildings located downhill to the east were a stable for the dray animals (mules and horses used for hauling wagons), teamster quarters, forage barn, and blacksmith shop, all four being constructed of log.

#33 Colonel H. Boyd McKeen. *Courtesy Ted Dombroski, Co. K, 81st Pennsylvania Volunteer Infantry War Group.*

In the 1800s building standards were different from today. In today's world, we know about 2 inch x 4 inch boards and that wall lengths should be divisible by four due to sheets of plywood, gypsum board and insulating boards being four feet wide. Back then a support in a wall could have a 25-inch center then shift to an 11-inch center then back to a 29-inch center. It just depended upon the carpenter's need of where he thought a support should be located, unlike today's uniform16-inch centers. Thus, uniformity was not an issue so a building could be 25 feet wide instead of 24 feet or 28 feet like we have today.

Adjutant's Office size: 24 feet by 48 feet

The adjutant, usually a Lieutenant, served as the assistant to the Commanding Officer. He kept all the regiments records and served as commander when needed. The Adjutant handled all the administrative needs of the fort such as promotions, demotions, graves registration, passes, as well as all written orders. If it involved paperwork, more than likely it initiated from this office or ended up here. During payday this building was used for the disbursement of wages.

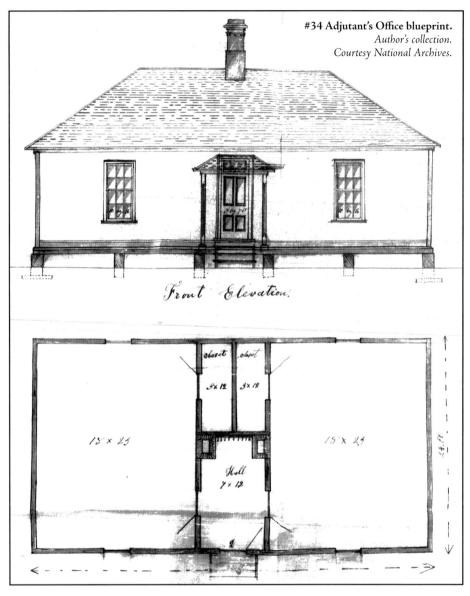

#34 Adjutant's Office blueprint.
Author's collection.
Courtesy National Archives.

Front Elevation.

#35 Adjutant's site.
Author's collection.

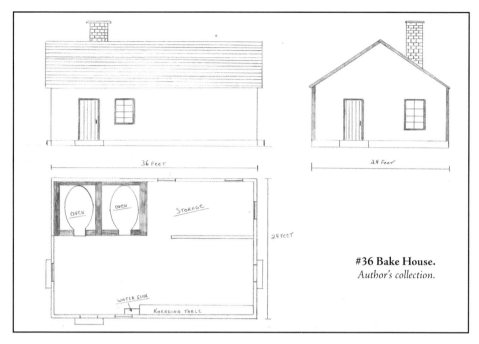

#36 Bake House.
Author's collection.

Bake House- size: 24 feet by 30 feet

The fort's bake house was where all the bread was made each day. Every soldier was allotted 16 ounces of bread per day, which took approximately 600 pounds of wheat and 40 gallons of water to produce enough bread for everyone at the fort each day. The bake house also made occasional pies when fruit was in season. The smell of bread must have been wonderful as it wafted through the open plains, but then it surely was torture inhaling that aroma and not being able to sample it immediately, even though fresh baked bread was not eaten because it was thought to be bad for one's health.

The bakery had to have been a great place to work during the winter months with two huge ovens cooking all day, but it must have been miserable during the summer months wearing wool uniforms. Many unwanted visitors went to the bakery throughout the day, either for the warmth or handouts, especially at the Infantry Post's baker since it was located next to the schoolhouse.

#37 Bake House site. Author's collection.

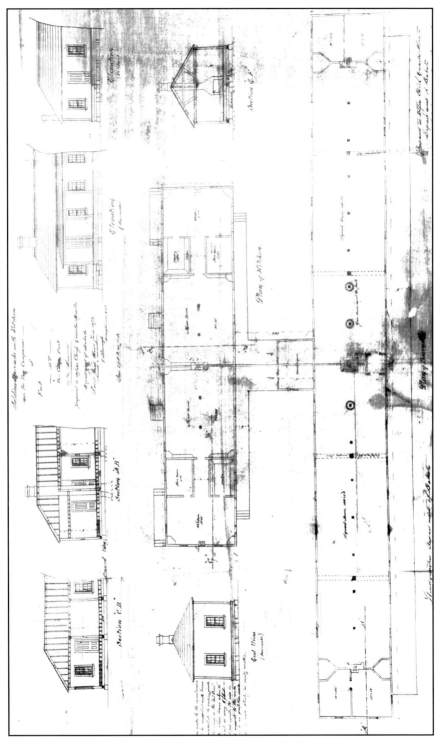

#38 Barrack's blueprint. *Author's collection. Courtesy National Archives.*

Barracks- size: 24 feet by 232 feet, barracks area 24 feet by 26 feet, washing area 24 feet by 119 feet

This unusually shaped building housed the enlisted men as well as the company's 1st Sergeants and Company Clerks. It could billet 88 men and their equipment comfortably. The 1st Sergeant and Clerk's Quarters, which had a bedroom and small office were located at each end on the main building

Upon exiting the back door of the barracks one would see a 24 foot by 26 foot addition that attached the barracks to the mess hall. This room was used for their daily toilet of brushing teeth and washing using ewers,, pitchers of water and bowls. The mess hall had a common dining area with a kitchen and storeroom on each end. Both kitchen/storeroom areas had a cistern dug below them for the storage of fruits and vegetables. As previously mentioned, this barracks also had a third cistern lined with rocks located below the wash area between the barracks and the mess hall. This may indicate that this particular cistern was used more for a bombproof than for food storage alone.

#40 Barrack's Cistern. *Author's collection.*

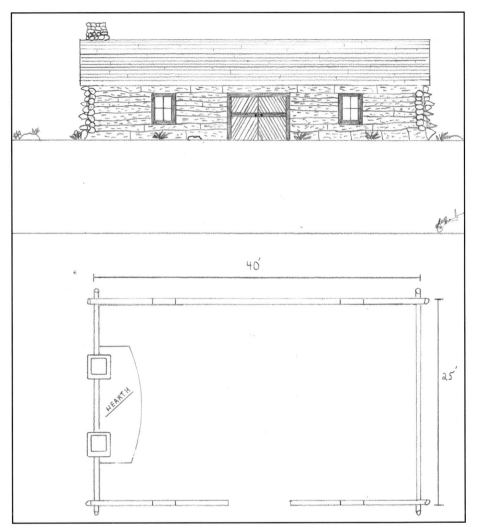

#41 What the Blacksmith Shop may have looked like. *Author's collection.*

Blacksmith shop- size: 24 feet by 40 feet

Constructed of log this building was where the blacksmith made chains, knives, hinges, nails, tools, horseshoes, hooks, wagon parts, pots and pans, andirons (metal supports for the logs in a fireplace), and wheel rims. The term "blacksmith" has an interesting beginning. It brings to mind a picture of a huge, sweaty man, covered with black soot on his face, arms, and leather bib apron, hammering away on a glowing piece of metal propped on his anvil as a resounding ping echoes throughout, each time the hammer strikes.

That is pretty close to what it was like. However the term "blacksmith" does not refer to the black soot prevalent on the man. "Black" refers to the iron metal with its layers of dark oxide that formed on the metal during smelting and forming. The "smith" term has two possible origins. The first, being anyone who worked with sharp tools. The second, from the word "smite", which means to strike. Either way, through colloquialism the two words became one…"blacksmith."

#42 Site of
Blacksmith's
forge at Fort
Lincoln.
*Courtesy State
Historical
Society
of North
Dakota,*
0105-027

#43 What the Blacksmith's Shop interior may have looked like. *Courtesy Barry Martin.*

A blacksmith formed his metal items by placing the crude iron in a hearth of glowing embers of coke, coal or wood. Using a huge leather bellows or a hand cranked mechanism, he forced air into the coals creating a hotter ember that heated the iron into a red hot glowing firebrand. This hot metal then became more malleable so the smithy could then form it into the desired shape by hammering it upon his anvil. Once shaped, the item could be hardened by heating it back to a cherry-red color, and then immersing it in water. This process was known as "quenching." The smithy was responsible for repairs on any metal as well as designing and fabricating new tools or implements. Here is another building that must have had many unscheduled visitors during the winter months. The blacksmith was the hardware store of the 19th Century.

#44 Block House with sentry at Fort Lincoln.
Courtesy State Historical Society of North Dakota, A5828

Blockhouses- size: 24 feet by 24 feet

The purpose of a blockhouse was to afford protection for the fort by giving it a solid almost impenetrable structure to fight from as well as offering the sentries an unobstructed view to better see opposing forces. There were 3 blockhouses, three stories tall. They appear like two square boxes put on top of one another at a right angle with a spire of a box about the size of an outhouse on the roof. Gun ports were afforded five to a side. With the second story constructed at an angle on top of the first story, the blockhouse had eight sides. There was a single door on the bottom floor, which was bolted from the inside. There was a "sentry walk" on top of the second story roof around the structure so that the sentry was given a 360-degree view of the surrounding terrain. Directly in the center of the roof was a sentry box with gun ports on all four sides where the soldier on guard could be protected from the elements as well as being able to shoot from its elevation should the fort be under attack. This sentry box was also the access to the stairway that went directly down the center of the building. The stairwell also served the purpose of housing the stovepipe for the small pot bellied stove on the ground floor.

The soldiers on guard duty were assigned for two hours (plus or minus depending upon the weather). At every hour the guard would report out loud that all was well then the closest blockhouse would then echo this verbal report, if applicable. Thus it would go around the entire fort alerting everyone to the conditions of safety at the moment. Visiting a blockhouse is a must. Once on top it becomes apparent why this location was decided upon for the fort. One can see for miles in any direction and with the depleted trees and foliage of the 1800's the protecting view must have been ideal for the guards.

Boarding House- size: unknown

The boarding house was located on the road going up to the Infantry Post and served as housing for visitors to the fort or those passing through to points further west. It has been asked if it was a government boarding house since it was based on a federal reserve. In the 19th century different criteria existed for businesses and buildings. If a

#45 Breastwork's Gatling Gun Crew. *Courtesy State Historical Society of North Dakota, 00900-31*

private owner of a business received approval from Division Headquarters or from the commanding officer, a business could be constructed on the fort's reserve. This boarding house was privately owned and may have been used by visitors to the area just passing through at the stage stop located at the post office.

Breastwork- size: 16 feet by 140 feet

Breastworks are defensive structures to protect the soldiers during combat. The equipment utilized to construct the breastwork depended upon the materials available. Most were made from mounds of dirt piled between the soldiers and their enemy. It became a common practice to fill cloth bags full of dirt, often called "sandbags", which would absorb the impact of the projectiles fired and prevent them from passing through to harm the defending soldiers. Other breastworks could also be ditches dug into the ground so that the soldier was not visible to the enemy during battle, offering protection much like that of a rifle pit,

#46 Breastwork site (where trees are located on top of hill). *Author's collection.*

often called a "fox hole." On the west side of the Infantry Post, approximately 520 feet from the southwest blockhouse, was a fortified breastworks, which overlooked the sloping plains. The earth was excavated 16 feet wide in a lazy horseshoe shape 140 feet long. The excavated earth was packed into sandbags then stacked in front of the gun offering a protective wall between the Indians and the artillerymen. The Gatling guns covered the more easily assaulted land to prevent raids or attacks by Indian forces. When manned, a Gatling gun could lay down a barrage of fire that would normally take dozens of soldiers to shoot. The main weakness of a Gatling gun was its propensity to jam due to overheating, which occurred because there was no way of cooling the gun barrels.

Carpenter shop- size: Unknown

The carpenter shop had to have been the busiest crew on post. Carpenters were responsible for anything to do with wood, with the exception of making wheels. Since the fort's structures were constructed entirely out of wood, the carpenters built any buildings needed at the fort. The carpenters also made window frames, doors, coffins, grave markers, sheds, and all repairs on wood items.

#47 Carpenter Shop site. *Author's collection.*

#48 What the carpenter shop may have looked like. Courtesy Barry Martin.

#49 Cemetery. *Author's collection.*

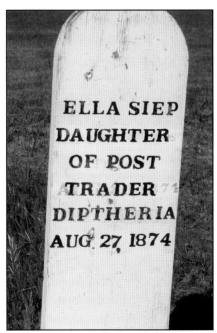

#50 Cemetery marker. *Author's collection*

ELLA SIEP DAUGHTER OF POST TRADER DIPTHERIA AUG 27 1874

Cemetery- size: 200 feet by 600 feet

Further west of the breastworks is the fort cemetery which is built upon a useless piece of ground. It has been questioned why the location was chosen given the hundreds of acres with more level terrain in which to inter the dead. When viewed today the topography of the cemetery is so terrible that if the graves were dug north to south, the deceased would almost be standing up. The cemetery in the 1880s had 41 souls buried there (one being female, the Sutlers' daughter who died of diphtheria). The deaths vary from drowning and disease to shootings in town. No one is interred there now due to federal dictate stating a federal cemetery must have a flag flying over it at all times. When the fort was decommissioned there was no longer anyone to tend the flag so the bodies were disinterred and buried at other cemeteries. The soldiers were reburied at Custer National Cemetery at the Little Big Horn Battlefield in Crow Agency, Montana. The civilians who were unclaimed were reburied at the Greenwood, Cemetery in Mandan, North Dakota.

#51 Cemetery marker. *Author's collection.*

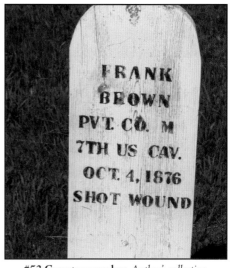

#53 Cemetery marker. *Author's collection.*

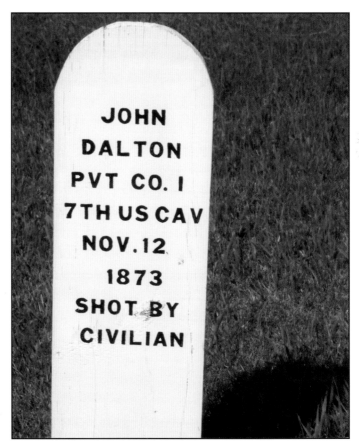

#52 Cemetery marker.
Author's collection.

#54 Commissary site.
Author's collection.

Commissary- size: 25 feet by 124 feet

The commissary basically was responsible for receiving, superintending and issuing of the fort's food supplies. The Commissary and Quartermaster had to have great integrity because they were responsible for supplies entering the fort as well as their distribution. They had to be skilled in reading, writing and math, and be able to keep accurate records. Both positions were appointed by the commanding officer. The commissary also oversaw anything to do with the cooks. The building held all foodstuffs in crates, barrels, tins or cloth sacks, which were later distributed to the appropriate companies with all the necessary paperwork covering the transactions. The soldiers working in the commissary storehouse handled the drawing and distribution of rations, were responsible for the feeding, care, and slaughter of all cattle, they made sure the rotation of supplies was performed properly to avoid spoiling, as well as making sure the salted meat barrels were rolled over to prevent the meat from drying out due to the air pocket inside. Another responsibility was the proper care of the scales and weights used in the disbursement of food supplies. This commissary had a full-length basement/storage area beneath the building. This was a must since it stored perishable food and it would maintain the freshness of the food much longer than being in the heat or cold.

Dead House- size: 16 feet by 16 feet

The "dead house" is what we commonly refer to as the morgue. It had four walls without windows, a door, roof and maybe wooden benches to place the body on. It was nothing like the morgues we have today with medical supplies, powerful lights or laboratory equipment. There were no embalming procedures, thus a body began decaying immediately. With no refrigeration, the bacteria grew rapidly in the summer months emitting the tell-tale odor of putrification. This is how the tradition of placing flowers around a coffin came about. Flowers were arranged around the deceased to mask the odor of the decaying body. The dead house was basically just a storage building for bodies until a hole in the ground could be dug. Sometimes this delay could take months due to the frozen earth of winter. This may sound archaic, but in fact, even today small towns in northern states who can't afford the expensive equipment needed to dig through three to four feet of frozen ground follow this practice. The local funeral homes store the bodies in caskets until the earth thaws out enough to dig.

#55 Dead House (framed structure on right).
Courtesy State Historical Society of North Dakota,00739-V1-p58e

The identification of the dead house in this photo may be incorrect. It lists the small, framed structure to the right of the log building as the morgue/dead house. Though it is about the size of a dead house its location in the photo is questionable. Fort Lincoln's Historian places the dead house location approximately 30 feet northeast of the hospital, which is more likely to be correct since it was customary for the dead houses to be constructed fairly close to the hospitals for convenience. The reason for the concerned discrepancy in the photo is the terrain. The terrain in the photo and the terrain around the hospitals are so blatantly different. As can be seen in the photo the designated dead house on the right is built on a stilt foundation next to a very steep decline. Both hospitals at Fort Lincoln were built on relatively flat ground so this may dispel the identification of

#56 Rick Chambers global positioning the Dead House site.
Author's collection.

this structure as a dead house. Though the photo doesn't match up with the terrain around either hospital, it matches up perfectly with the terrain near the scout's quarters.

The only buildings on top of the hill constructed of logs were the laundress quarters, which was 30 feet by 180 feet and the three scout's quarters, which were approximately 20 feet by 30 feet (approximately the size of the log building in the photo). They were also built upon or near the crest of the hill. If this is a scout's quarters, it is highly improbable they would have built a dead house within a few feet of it, especially if it was an Indian scout's quarters.

With its narrow, square construction, unusually high roof, no windows, stilt base, and being adjacent to a scout's quarters it is believed that this structure may have been used to hang fresh game such as deer or antelope. If this is the case, then in actuality it was in fact a dead house, just not one for soldiers.

Ferry Landing- size: unknown

The ferry landing east of the post trader was the landing site for three steamboats, the *Denver*, the *Union* and of course the *Far West*. The *Denver* and *Union* were used to ferry across the river to Bismarck or Whiskey Point or for short excursions up and down the river. These two ships had seen better days and were not very reliable according to Libby Custer. This was not an elaborate landing, just a dirt ramp cut into the natural earth berm to facilitate the loading and unloading of wagons and horses.

The *Far West* was used as a long-distance ship because it was larger and in better condition than either the *Union* or the *Denver*. The *Far West* has become one of the most famous paddle wheelers due to it being used by Generals Terry, Gibbon and Custer for the ill-fated Little Big Horn Campaign. The *Far West* was thrust into infamy because it carried the wounded troopers back to Fort Lincoln. Captain Marsh, who ferried the troopers, had also been the captain on the *Denver* as well as working with Mark Twain aboard the *A. B. Chambers* on the Missouri River.

The Ferry Landing can be seen (in photo #6 on page 13) on the left of the photo, situated above the long building that was the Wheelwright's shop.

#57 Ferry landing. *Courtesy State Historical Society of North Dakota, A5621*

Forage Barn- size: unknown

This building was constructed of logs and held hay, straw, and grain for the dray animals. Basically this building was nothing more than four walls and a roof. If the log walls were tightly fitted, as in the photo it would be necessary to create ventilation doors (as shown) throughout the building. However, if the

#58 Forage Barn vent doors. *Author's collection.*

log walls were more loosely constructed, the gaps between the logs would provide the necessary air flow to prevent the lethal explosive gases from accumulating.

Gun Emplacement- size: approximately 11 feet by 33 feet

Information is lacking concerning this gun emplacement north of the breastworks. Why it was located so near other breastworks is a mystery. It may have given protection further down the hill from marauding Indians but it was still an area that the other breastworks could have covered. There are so many unreasonable placements of

#59 Gun emplacement crew. *Courtesy State Historical Society of North Dakota, C0895*

#60 Gun emplacement site (where grass is flattened). *Author's collection.*

buildings throughout this fort that do not make sense from a protection standpoint of military installations, especially with continued sporadic attacks on the fort.

Hospital- size: 44 feet by 152 feet, main building; 16 feet by 40 feet, rear wing

The concept of the "modern" hospital had just come of age a mere ten years earlier. Until then a military hospital was a place to store the infirmed until they were better or dead. Hospitals were demoralizing as well as spawning grounds for infections and disease. Being placed in a military hospital was considered a last home for the patients. With small structures, fetid air, unsanitary conditions and rudimentary care a hospital was a mere staging area for the dead house, instead of an institute for healing.

Then military hospital reform came about. New hospitals were constructed with wide-open designs with less opportunity for dirt and filth to accumulate as well as allowing in the healthy beneficial air they knew would help the patients. The interiors were white washed to aid in illumination while offering the appearance of cleanliness and health. White wash also had another side effect; it was made from lime and water, sometimes mixed with glue to make it adhere better. Lime prevents the growth of bacteria so it was an ideal mixture to place upon hospital walls. Another phase of construction was to try and erect the hospitals as close to rivers and lakes for the fresh breezes as well as the mental aesthetics they helped provide.

The hospital must have been the most interesting building in the entire fort because of its "modern" innovations. It had a central two-story structure with two, single story wards on either side of the main structure. In back there was

#61 Hospital. Courtesy State Historical Society of North Dakota, B0376

another two-story addition containing the kitchen, matron's room, offices, etc. There was a wrap around, roofed veranda accenting the hospital where patients could sit in chairs or even lie in beds to inhale the "healing vapors" of the outdoors. The original blueprints show only one ward, but an additional ward was added. The blueprints were not always followed and could have items added or deleted, depending on the

#62 Hospital site. *Author's collection.*

needs of each fort, such as the cupola shown in the photo above.

On top of each ward room was a running cupola that ran almost the entire length of the ward. Small windows were placed the length of this cupola giving the much needed light as well as fresh air, like an archaic solarium. Inside the two wards were two "water closets." The term "water closet" is a misnomer since water was a viable commodity and could not be used to flush away human waste. The flushable toilet as we know it would not be invented for another decade, but in the original blueprints there are two small rooms marked "W. C." A true water closet consisted of the waste dropping into a sloped trough. As more waste was accumulated on the trough or the odor became unbearable, water would be poured into the trough carrying the waste away to a collection vat. The vat would then be emptied later.

With the advent of new hospital construction even the lowly water closet was given a new makeover. These nine-foot by nine-foot rooms were given two, three-foot by six-foot windows for ventilation. Whether the human act of voiding oneself was done using a bedpan, chamber pot or earth closet is unknown but it was surely done indoors in the wards. An earth closet is a holed seat with a bin of dirt below it. When finished the person would cover the excrement with dirt, ashes or whatever was available.

One cannot appreciate the design of this building by looking at the photos or the blueprints. When a model was constructed of the hospital it showed a very aesthetic looking building with beautiful lines melding into one another.

Ice houses- size: approximately 48 feet by 48 feet

The ice houses could be constructed of various materials in various ways. Some may be framed structures with sawdust between the walls used for insulation, or they could be constructed entirely out of logs. A third option was to use a natural hillside for two or three of the walls, then construct the remaining walls of wood. The ice would then be lowered into the icehouse then layered with straw or sawdust between the blocks of ice to prevent them from melting together into

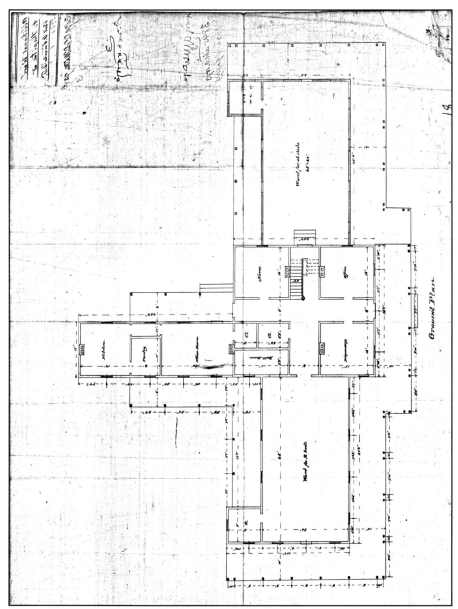

#63 Hospital floor plan blueprint. Author's collection. *Courtesy National Archives.*

one hug block. Once filled, a roof would be constructed over it, then bermed with soil for further insulation. Either way the icehouses would hold tons of ice. The hard work would be appreciated later in the summer months when it would be used to preserve meat acquired during hunts, ice for cooling drinks, or used in the hospital for the patients.

In photo #6, the two buildings to the upper left, along the river may be the Ice Houses.

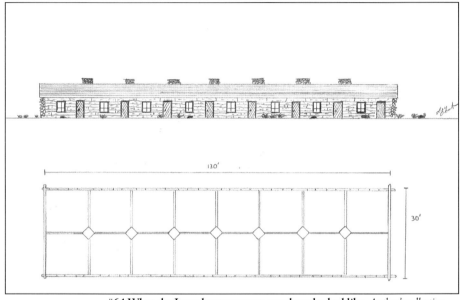

#64 What the Laundress quarters may have looked like. *Author's collection.*

#65 Laundress Quarters site. *Author's collection.*

Laundress Quarters- size: 30 feet by 120 feet

The laundress quarters was constructed of log and housed up to 16 laundresses. Some laundresses had families and would use their daughters, such as the pretty miss below, to help with the grueling work. In actuality the process of washing clothes was a laborious, painful existence. Besides having to pour buckets of water into some type of vessel for heating, they would then have to pour the heated water into either a wooden or zinc coated tub. Washing required them to stand hunched over the tubs scrubbing clothes for hours on end each day. The act of scrubbing the clothing on a corrugated wash board must have been painful by the end of the day. They had to constantly grasp and squeeze the material as they rubbed it back and forth over the wash board. Once cleaned, they had to wring and twist the clothes to get rid of the excess water and soap, then repeat the process for rinsing the clothes, before hanging them out to dry. In our modern age we complain about wrist and hand pain due to using the mouse of our computer as our wrist rests upon a pad. From this over-exertion we contract carpel tunnel syndrome and complain about the hardships of the job. To add to the discomfort and pain, the laundresses had to deal with the harsh lye soap that dehydrated their skin of its natural oils, causing the skin to become red, tender, and rough from the constant contact with the lye used in the soap. Lye being caustic would destroy the skin cells, which caused the skin to peel and crack, which would make the hands bleed.

Soap has two ingredients, lye and lard. Lye is made by filtering water through the ashes of burnt wood. Lard is made from rendering animal fat (melting down the fat by heating it) called adamantine or tallow, which is also used to make candles. The lard and water were boiled over a fire until the substance became a gooey consistency. When the goo was "stiff" enough to hold the stirring spatula upright unattended it was finished. The concoction was then poured into molds of a more manageable size and allowed to harden by drying. Viola...lye soap.

#66 Miss Maddy (Laundress' daughter doing the laundry). *Author's collection.*

#67 Mandan Mound. *Author's collection.*

Mandan Mounds- size: various, usually 30 feet in diameter

In the fort parameters is the area inhabited by the Mandan Indians. The Mandans arrived at the junction of the Heart and Missouri rivers in the early 1500s. Called the "On-Slant Village" because of it being built on a hillside, it fell into ruins by the time Lewis and Clark arrived in 1804. Decimated by smallpox through the years, the Mandan population shrank to less than 300 in less than 100 years after inhabiting the area, though at one time it was estimated that there were over 15,000 warriors.

The Mandan Mounds were an earth house averaging 30 to 40 feet in diameter and standing 10 feet high in the center. The ceremonial lodges were almost 90 feet in diameter. They were built by constructing a framework of large logs, then covered with interlaced branches, and finally with grass and dirt. The lodges were warm in the winter and cool in the summer with this type of construction. The sleeping area was on the outside walls, with a fire pit in the center of the floor and a hole in the roof which allowed most of the smoke to exit.

Though a peaceful tribe, they knew they had to protect themselves from raids by other tribes. The east side of the village was protected by a steep wash bank of the Missouri River, and the south side was protected by a deep coulee (steep-sided ravine). The only defensive system they had to construct was a ditch and a palisade near it, located on the northwest side of the village.

Officer's Quarters- size: 48 feet by 60 feet

The four Officers' Quarters were duplexes, thus making a total of eight residences. They were similar in design to the Cavalry Officer Quarters but only one story tall and very rudimentary with only the bare necessities needed for the protection from the elements. The appearance of the buildings was deceiving. The interior walls and ceilings were not plastered lathing, instead they were covered with very thick paper similar to cardboard.

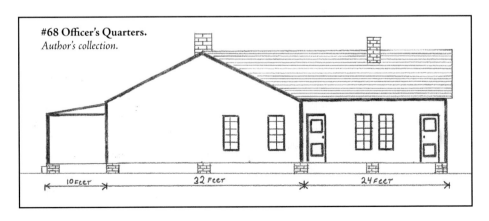

#68 Officer's Quarters. *Author's collection.*

10 Feet   32 Feet   24 Feet

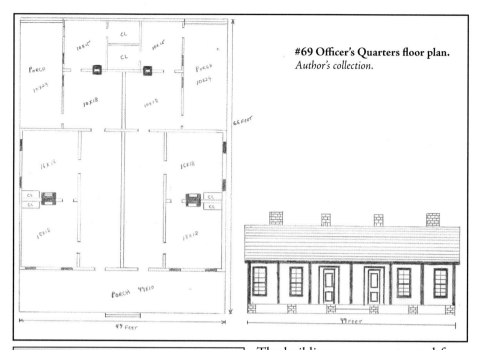

#69 Officer's Quarters floor plan.
Author's collection.

#70 Officer's Quarters sites. *Author's collection.*

The buildings were constructed from local cottonwood trees freshly cut down then immediately made into lumber. By not allowing the lumber to season (dry out), it warped as it dried, especially when heat from the fireplaces was used during the colder months. This warping created gaps between the boards, allowing the cold air to blow in during the winter months and the mosquitoes to invade during the summertime. During the winter some innovative officers would hang canvas over the walls, creating an air pocket and reducing drafts, thus making the interior warmer.

Though inappropriately constructed, at least the officers had privacy with their family. Should there be unmarried officers, they would "bach" it with other unmarried officers. These quarters would then be designated as, "Bachelor Officer Quarters." Residency was based upon rank and the availability of quarters. Should an officer with more rank desire to live in one of the inhabited quarters, he could oust the junior officer even if the junior officer had a family. This custom was referred to as "ranking out." To us this does not seem fair but living space was at a premium. There did not seem to be any harsh feelings with this practice even when one family was forced to live in a converted chicken coop due to being ranked out by a superior officer who was a bachelor.[18] Over time commanding officers would allow additions to be built to the original quarters to facilitate needs or desires. This practice happened so frequently that few of the quarters resembled one another.

#71 Palisade. Courtesy State Historical Society of North Dakota, 00200-5x7-523.

Palisades- size: 1,486 feet

The blockhouses were initially attached with two palisades running between them. Over time the need for the palisades diminished so the labor and time-consuming task of repair and replacement ceased. The palisade, stockade or fence, by whatever name it is called, was approximately 10 feet tall with battle ports spaced every so often so that a soldier could shoot out at attacking forces from behind the wall. One wall was 510 feet long and the other was 976 feet long. That is over 1,400 feet or more than ¼ mile long! The construction of the stockade must have been a huge undertaking, to cut and deliver the trees, not even mentioning the work to erect and then maintain the stockade through the years.

Post Office- size: unknown

The Post Office was the building used for receiving and sending mail and also contained the telegraph office, as well as being the stage stop. Its location was next to the Post Trader's Store.

In photo #5, the Post Office is to the far left foreground. It is partially hidden by a tree and the Post Trader's Store. In photo #6, the Post Office is located near the center of the photo but is again partially hidden by a tree and the Post Trader's Store.

#72 Post Office site. Author's collection.

#73 Post Trader Store (long building), post office is partially shown to the left.
Courtesy State Historical Society of North Dakota, A4406.

Post Trader- size: unknown

The Post Trader was a privately owned business that was approved and franchised by the Federal Government. The sutler (Post Trader) sold merchandise to the soldiers for cash or credit. His "sutler's check" was a $5 credit advance given to soldiers for goods purchased at his store that had to be repaid on the next payday. The store was a business containing an area to purchase various canned goods and dry goods. It also had two billiard table rooms, one for officers and one for enlisted men. There was also alcohol sold on the premises, with the stipulation that enlisted men must have the approval of their Commanding Officer.

The dry goods section was more like a small general store stocking only items the soldiers would be interested in purchasing. The sutler's prices were exorbitant, maybe charging two or three times the goods value. This price gouging was such a concern to Custer that he encouraged his troops to buy their needed items from town. He also had provisions and supplies purchased in town, and then sold them to the soldiers at

#74 Post Trader's interior.
Courtesy State Historical Society of North Dakota, A1080.

cost, thus boycotting the sutler. This practice was soon halted by Custer's superiors who ordered him to rescind this unapproved action.

Custer suspected graft and corruption throughout the post trader system all the way up to Secretary of War Belknap, and even President Grant's brother, Orville. Custer testified in Washington D. C. concerning this alleged corruption. As a result of his testimony and his disobeying orders to remain in Washington, Custer was arrested and detained, almost missing the Little Big Horn Campaign until intervention by Generals Terry and Sheridan.

In photo #5 the Post Trader Store is located to the far left. It is the long, light colored building. In photo #6 the Post Trader Store is on the left center of the photo. It can be distinguished by its long, light colored roof.

Powder House- size: 12 feet by 35 feet

There were three powder houses located on the south side of the infantry post that were buried into the hillside facing the cavalry post. Only one wall was exposed, which contained the doorway. The other three walls were built into the hill and the roof was bermed with earth. They were designed like a root cellar in appearance. The reason for burying them was a safety precaution. Should a powder house explode, the dirt would absorb the explosion and funnel the debris downhill away from the other buildings. A regular framed building would explode sending out thousands of projectiles and lethal splinters from the disintegrating building in a 360-degree field of mayhem. The powder houses had drainage systems to prevent the explosives from becoming wet from the rain as well as ventilation systems to keep the explosives from becoming damp from humidity or from building up explosive gases.

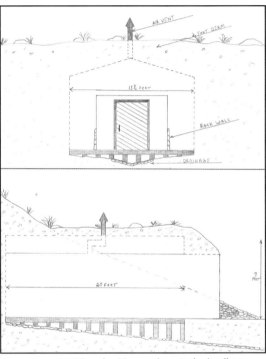

#75 Powder House plan. *Author's collection.*

#76 Powder House site. *Author's collection.*

Prehistoric Mound- size: various

This is not part of the fort, but it lies directly within its parameters. This mound reinforces the importance of Fort Mc Keen being constructed upon this hill.

There were three diverse cultures almost two thousand years apart that selected the same hill. The estimated date of this mound is 400 B.C. to 400 A. D. The mound system may have been built by the Hopewell Indians, who were known for

#77 **Prehistoric mound.** *Author's collection.*

building mounds. The purpose of this mound is unknown. Mounds were made for a variety of reasons: spiritual, burial, housing, or representing animal shapes. As can be seen, this mound is not a particular shape, other than a small rise in the terrain.

Privy- size: 5 feet by 10 feet

Outhouses were numerous throughout the fort. There was an estimated 100 of them at any one time. They were constructed of a uniform size since the military even had blue prints for them. At five feet by ten feet they were considered "4 holers," which meant, there were four holes in the seating portion of the privy.

Use of an outhouse is an experience. Not even today's "port-a-potties" can compare. Unlike the hospital, the privy was a breezy, smelly affair without a proper seat or lid. An oval hole was cut in the horizontal planking of the seating area. Today we have comfortable toilet seats and toilet paper. Back then anything could be used such as newspaper, paper, grass, leaves and even corncobs! They were cold in the winter, especially as one sat down on the wooden planking with the wind blowing from below, chilling the exposed derriere, but dangerous in the summer. Dangerous in the sense of having spiders crawl across bare buttocks or worse having hornets buzzing private parts! One sat alert looking for spiders and bees but it was the ones unseen that were dangerous.

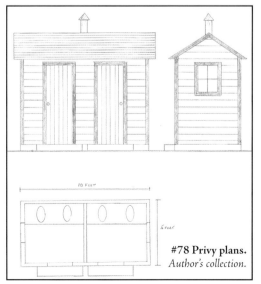

#78 **Privy plans.** *Author's collection.*

Archaeologists have found a treasure trove of information from outhouse pits. They can learn about the life of the persons who used them. The reason was the privy was also used to throw away small broken items that were no longer needed such as bottles, buttons, tin cans, broken pottery, etc. Another reason archaeologist look forward to excavating outhouses is, with today's technology they are able to determine the diets of the users thus disclosing the types of plants and animals of the area that were being used for food.

#79 Quartermaster site.
Author's collection.

Quartermaster's Storehouse- size: 25 feet by 124 feet

The Quartermaster was responsible for more supplies than the commissary. Until the construction of the Ordinance Depot, the Quartermaster stored all firearms, weapons and ammunition. The Quartermaster storehouse held most of the supplies needed by the fort such as clothing, weapons, bedding, nails, tools, saddles, garrison equipage, etc. Not only were the Quartermasters responsible for distribution of supplies, but they were in charge of inspecting and condemning property no longer useable.

The Quartermaster was responsible for procurement and distribution of forage, wood for heating and cooking, purchasing horses and wagons, construction of roads and buildings, and, while away from the fort on expeditions or patrols the erection of tents and pickets, the identity of all company animals and their proper car, and loading and unloading wagons. During battle, the Quartermaster looked after the wagons.

Residences- size: various

There were two private residences located at the fort. One is assumed to have been that of the Post Traders; there is uncertainty about who owned the other building.

#80 Rick Chambers pointing out one of the rifle pits that he and the author discovered.
Author's collection.

Rifle Pits- size: various

Rifle pits were scattered around the Infantry Post. Some were hundreds of feet or even thousands of feet from the protection of the blockhouses. In September of 2006 the author and his brother, Rick discovered four rifle pits around the Infantry Post that had been unknown about for years. Their location is kept secret to prevent damage until they can be excavated properly and professionally. These pits must have been dug fairly deep since over 130 years later they still remain approximately twelve inches deep and three feet in diameter. With over a century of erosion, the pits are still very discernable over the landscape. A rifle pit, also called a "fox hole," is a hole in the ground dug by a soldier to fight from during battle, while concealing him and offering as little view of himself as possible. The pits could be dug with an entrenching tool, knife, rifle butt, board, or anything that could move dirt to create an impression in the earth.

The pits had to have been more than a hole dug in the ground for protection during a sporadic heated battle. They were too large and too deep to have been dug using a knife, rifle butt or even a 19th century entrenching tool while being fired upon. (Of course we can only imagine how fast and deep one can dig while being attacked.) If they were in fact dug during a battle, they had to have been later modified to their larger size. Were they dug to protect the trails up to the post or were they forward observation posts? If used as observation posts it must have been a very lonely, frightening job knowing the skillful stealth abilities of the Indians.

Schoolhouse- size: 16 feet by 32 feet

The education of the soldier's children did not go unattended. In more affluent forts, officer's children and enlisted men's children would have separate schools. One thing they both would have in common was that they were one-room schoolhouses, where pupils of all ages were taught by one teacher. The teachers could have been officer's wives or daughters or even laundresses, depending upon who was available and had the most education. It was not uncommon in that century for teachers to be 14 to 18 years of age.

This school did not look like the prototypical one-room school we envision having a steep pitched roof and a bell tower looming over the top of the front door. This school was a single floor structure and rectangular in shape. The school houses were not only used as schools but may be used as a chapel, meeting room or used for parties and dances.

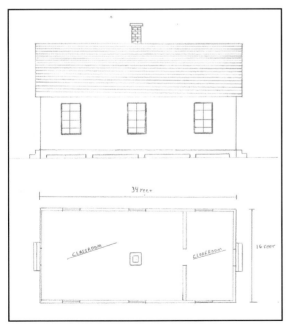

#81 What the school house may have looked like.
Author's collection.

#82 School House site. *Author's collection.*

Scouts' Quarters- size: various

The Scouts' quarters were also made of logs. Forget the thought of all log buildings being constructed with evenly dimensional logs. Instead, log buildings were built with what was available, giving them a homely, dilapidated appearance.

These quarters were afforded to all scouts, but were seldom used by the Indian scouts, who felt they couldn't breathe properly inside any building, so they used the quarters for storage and slept in their tipis (tepees) near the quarters. The log quarters were considered dark and dank, with bothersome odors according to some who visited the scouts; a preference developed for meeting the scouts outdoors. The offensive odor could be due to the lack of bathing, but more than likely it was the building's design. Made of logs with very low roofs, limited windows, and dirt floors, the air couldn't circulate properly. It must have been stifling, making prime conditions for mold and mushrooms.

#83 Scout's Quarters site. *Author's collection.*

Stable- size: unknown

This stable was built of logs and it housed the dray animals, which were horses and mules used for hauling the wagons. Though not built as well as the Cavalry Post stables, which were built with frame construction, this building performed its purpose well: the protection of the animals from the elements and theft.

Steam Mill- size: unknown

The steam mill was similar to the saw mill, with one exception. It was operated by a steam engine connected by belts to saws, edgers, and planers. The processing of lumber was faster and more proficient, and the edgers and planers made a smoother finish.

#84 Stable site. *Author's collection.*

#85 What the Steam Mill may have looked like. *Courtesy Barry Martin.*

#86 What interior of Steam Mill may have looked like. *Courtesy Barry Martin.*

Sundial- size: various

This instrument kept track of time by a pointer and the hours of the day arranged similar to a clock face. When the sun hit the pointer above the face, it cast a shadow upon the dial revealing the time of day. The exact location is unknown today, but it is assumed to have been behind the hospital. Most sundials are placed upon a high, unobstructed elevation. At the Infantry Post, this location would have been the prehistoric mound near the northeast blockhouse.

#87 Sun Dial. *Courtesy Lisa Hale*

Teamster Quarters- size: unknown

This log building was the living quarters for the men who drove the wagons. Teamsters, as they were called, were a rough group of people. Their normal everyday conversations were peppered with profanities, which only worsened when controlling their wagon teams. The skills it took to handle multi-animal teams were a gift. The knowledge required in hooking up and maintaining the myriad of leather straps, hooks, single trees or double trees (the wooden poles where the harness attached) could be confusing. Also, there was the knowledge needed to use the reins properly to steer the animals. Most people could not hitch up a team of horses to a wagon or even drive them once they were teamed.

It was also important to be able to read an animal's disposition and ability. This sense could make the difference between a team functioning well or trying to override or fight each other. The latter would cause delays, wear down the animals quickly, and create hardships for the teamster. If animals were not teamed properly, one side could pull more forcefully than the opposing side and break the single tree located between them. When the soldiers or the cavalry were at drill practice, teamsters were also at drill with their teams and wagons. The teamster was responsible for learning the commands and drills necessary to control the wagons during military maneuvers, such as going from a single file to two or four wagons abreast, then performing a perfunctory turn in an orderly fashion while in the multiple-wagon lines. They also practiced corralling (placing the wagons into a temporary corral using the wagons as fencing to keep mules or horses from wandering off or being stolen while on patrol or expeditions), hitching and unhitching, or loading and unloading the wagons. Their constant practice would save time while under attack or during a forced march.

Unknown Structures- size: A, 25 feet by 72 feet; B, 20 feet by 24 feet; C, 46 feet by 46 feet

The first unknown structure is immediately to the east of the blockhouse. The second unknown structure is just south west of the same blockhouse. We

#88 Unknown building site # A. *Author's collection.*

are unsure of its purpose. It was less than half the size of unknown structure #A.) The third unknown structure is also an enigma. Why is it located so far away from protection? It was a square building north of the gun emplacement site. The problem with most unknown buildings is that they were considered unimportant as far as survival or strategy and they felt it was not necessary to maintain records of the buildings purpose. Like most unknown buildings it just becomes relegated to being designated as…"possibly a storage building." A few of the unknown buildings may have been a wagon shed, wagon and carriage shed, quartermaster wagon shed, or a gun shed, all of which were at Fort Lincoln but the locations are unknown.

Wheelwright- size: unknown

The wheelwright was a true artisan and craftsman. His knowledge of wood was immeasurable because he had to understand what pressures the various types of wood could withstand. He had to know the correct wood to use such as using oak and not pine or cottonwood, in making the spokes of the wheel. He had to know what woods could be bent and which ones would split. The main job of the wheelwright was to cut, shape and join woods to make spokes, hubs and wheel rims as well as repairing wheels and wagons.

In photo #6, the Wheelwright is located on the far left foreground. It is the building with the long, light colored roof.

#89 Wheelwright site. *Author's collection.*

Chapter 3

Cavalry Post Structures

The nucleus of the Cavalry Post consisted of the commanding officer's quarters, 6 officer quarters, 3 enlisted men's barracks with attached mess, commissary, quartermaster storehouse, 2 granaries, dispensary, guard house, band quarters with attached mess, Non-commissioned Officer's quarters and the adjutant's office. Inside this mass of buildings known as "Cavalry Square" was a parade ground, which measured approximately 590 feet by 900 feet.

To the east of cavalry square was another set of buildings consisting of 7 stables and the laundress quarters. Buildings associated with the cavalry post were a theatre, ice houses, saw mill, hospital, dead house, hospital steward's quarters, officer's club, bake house, school/chapel, workshop, scout's quarters, powder magazine, commissary sergeant quarters, an extra stable, corral, root cellar, photo studio, tepees, as well as a few unknown buildings. To the southwest of the cavalry square were the ordinance storage, ordinance stable, ordinance depot, ordinance officer quarters, ordinance carpenter, ordinance barracks, and the ordinance office/workshop. The buildings at the fort were not constructed at one time, but rather, were built according to needs and desires. Nor were the buildings all standing at the same time. Some were lost to fire or were dismantled as others were being added.

Troopers were not generally big men. The average height was 5' 8" tall and weighed 150 lbs. When we look at the size of their boots they seem to be mere children, with most boots only being a size 8.

In comparison, the animals went through a more thorough examination than the soldiers. With the armament and supplies the trooper carried, averaging around 50 pounds, together with 15 pounds of grain, the horses had about 215 pounds on their back. Besides height and weight, if a man's heart was beating most of the time, and he had all his limbs, he would be deemed fit for military service. The cavalry soldiers did have one degenerative ailment that was inherent with cavalrymen. Today, as the skeletons of soldiers are discovered and examined they are able to determine that the individual was a horse soldier by his compressed spinal column due to all the traveling in the saddle.

The height of a horse was measured to the withers of the horse (withers are the bony projections near the base of the neck). The accepted height was set at 14.2 hands to 15.2 hands. A hand equals 4 inches, making the height of the horse's withers approximately 4 feet 8 inches to 5 feet tall. The standard weight of the horse was set at 1,000 pounds. Before purchase by the military, the horses were thoroughly examined by an experienced soldier and veterinarian and only the best of the lot were purchased. With a grading system the horses were branded with a "C" for cavalry use or with an "A" for use in the artillery, hauling cannons, limbers, or caissons. There was even a specification on how fast and how far a horse must be able to travel. An average speed for the horses on patrol was set at 6 to 6 ½ miles per hour and they must be able to walk 30 to 35 miles in a day. Mules were also subjected to a grading system upon purchase. They were branded with a "P" as a pack mule or a "W" to designate them for wagon use.

#90 Cavalry Post Buildings. *Author's collection.*

The most important thing a trooper had to do was take care of his mount. The horse was fed, watered and groomed before the trooper ate in the morning, and at night the horse was fed, watered, groomed and bedded down before the trooper retired for the night. Basically the horse came first in all accounts and the trooper who failed to follow this rule would rue the day he didn't take care of his horse, as he would be punished for his lack of concern.

Throughout time the horses and mules would wane in their ability through age or injuries. Often these unwanted animals would be designated for use in the Quartermaster Corps. These animals were used for hauling short distances or for everyday use about the post for various duties including messenger service or some as scouting mounts. Once assigned to the Quartermaster Corps, they were no longer well maintained or even kept clean since it was accepted that it was just a matter of time before the animal's demise. There were also times when horses or mules would be used as direly needed food for the soldiers while out on patrol after running out of food supplies. In actuality horse meat is not bad, but mule meat is stringy, tough, and chewy. When a horse was to be taken out of service it was branded on the left fore shoulder with an "IC," which stood for Inspected and Condemned.

#91 Adjutant's Office site. *Author's collection.*

#92 Bake House site. *Author's collection.*

Adjutant's Office- size: 24 feet by 48 feet

This building served the same purpose as the Adjutant's Office at the Infantry Post. This was the office of Lieutenant Cooke, who was killed at the Battle of the Little Big Horn. In photo #5, the Adjutant's Office is the small building immediately to the right of the topmost barracks. In photo #8, the Adjutant's Office is located between the Barracks and the Quartermaster Storehouse.

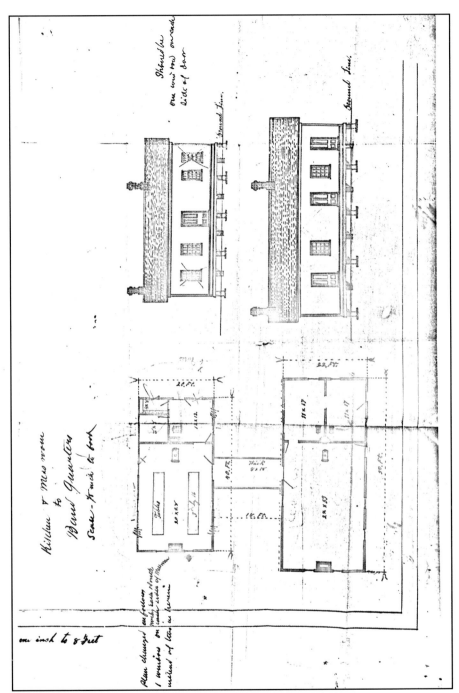

#93 Band Quarters blueprint. Author's collection. *Courtesy National Archives.*

In photo #5, the Band Quarters can be seen immediately to the left of the foremost Barracks. In photo #9, the Band Quarters can be seen on the right, it being the small light-colored building.

Bake House- size: 24 feet by 30 feet

This bake house served the same purpose as the infantry post. Its location was to the north of the stables. Except for the ovens, this building was very basic inside. Two huge brick ovens took up the majority of the space with a dry sink (a sink with no water pump or faucet) and a mixing/kneading trough or table that stood about three feet tall. A mixing/kneading trough was similar to a long, narrow wooden horse water trough you see in the westerns. The trough would be about four feet long, 18 inches wide and a foot deep. The ingredients for the bread were placed in the trough then manually mixed by hand, then kneaded by folding the dough repeatedly into itself thoroughly. This box made it easier to handle the bulky dough as well as preventing ingredients being spilled onto the floor. As if that really mattered to them during that time period.

Band Quarters- size: 23 feet by 50 feet (barracks), 8 feet by 8 feet (walkway), 23 feet by 40 feet (mess hall)

The band quarters had 8 rooms, housing at least 16 band members. It was similar in design as the barracks but much smaller. It too had an attached mess hall like the enlisted men's barracks, but instead of having a washhouse between them it just had a walkway between the quarters and mess hall.

The official nickname of the band was "Garry Owen." This was derived from the song, Garrai Eoin ("Owen's Garden"), that Custer loved so much. It was an Irish drinking song from the 17th Century Royal Irish Brigade that inspired them. Custer enjoyed music so much that the 7th Cavalry was the only U.S. Cavalry Regiment to have a band during the 1870's. Band members had other privileges besides their own quarters. Members were not expected to perform guard duty or fatigue duty.

Despite this favored status, there was one winter that Custer had problems with his band members while out on patrol. Due to the cold, the band decided they could no longer play their instruments. Mysteriously some of the instruments were either broken or the band members reported them too frozen to be played. Initially Custer put up with this lack of music from his favored troopers but eventually he decided to break up this minor revolt. He ordered all band members to begin working guard duties and fatigue duties while in the frigid cold.[19] Miraculously all instruments became repaired and were able to play the music Custer loved so much.

#94 7th Cavalry Band. *Author's collection.*

#95 Barracks. *Courtesy State Historical Society of North Dakota, A3113*

#96 Barracks front. *Author's collection.*

Barracks- size: 24 feet by 232 feet (barracks), 24 feet by 26 feet (washing area), 24 feet by 119 feet (mess hall)

The barracks buildings were the same size and design as the Infantry Posts. The barracks were designed to billet 44 men per wing, giving a manned compliment of 88 men per barracks, comfortably. However the number could be greater or smaller depending upon the staffing at the time. Each soldier had a footlocker at the base of his bunk for personal items, with pegs to store his property and a shelf on the wall at the head of the bed. Located in the middle isle of the barracks was a pot bellied stove and around the roof support beams were rifle racks. A fireplace stood at the ends of each barracks. An old adage comes out, "R.H.I.P." (Rank Has Its Privileges). This meant those with the highest rank or seniority got the prime bunks nearest the stoves during the winter months.

The mess hall addition was deceptive. It was actually two dining areas and two kitchens. The kitchens, storerooms and cisterns were located at the ends of the structure with the two dining rooms in the center separated by a duel fireplace. Also deceptive was the washing area. The section of building connecting the barracks and the mess hall had two washing areas, one for each barracks wing.

#97 Barracks side. *Author's collection.*

#98 2nd Barracks site. *Author's collection.*

#99 Barrack's interior. *Author's collection.*

#100 Barrack's interior. *Author's collection.*

#101 Barrack's 1st Sergeant's Quarters. *Author's collection.*

#102 Barrack's kitchen. *Author's collection.*

#103 Barrack's mess hall. *Author's collection.*

#104 Barrack's washing area. *Author's collection.*

Bath House- size: 16 feet by 39 feet

Blueprints were found for a bath house at Fort Lincoln. How many there were or even their location is a mystery. A policy did exist governing how often a soldier must bathe, but enforcement was lax due to either the availability of water or the lack of concern for hygiene. If Fort Lincoln had bathhouses it must have been a nice luxury. The bath house blueprints show a building that was made into two separate washing areas by a wall being placed in the center of the structure. A common chimney was shared, with each side having a separate fireplace/stove, two bathtubs and what appears to be an area designated for showering.

Most bathing was probably done in the river or by taking a "*sitz* bath" or "sponge bath." A *sitz* bath was a 2-and-a-half-foot, round, 20-gallon tub, similar in shape and size to a tin clothes-washing tub. A few alterations were done to the basic tub design to make it easier to use. The rim of the tub projected upward in the shape of a chair back while on the opposite side of the backing two "U" shaped notches were cut out of the side. When using a *sitz* bath, the bather sat in the tub with his back against the back of the tub while placing the legs in the notches, thus preventing the legs from having the circulation cut off by hanging them over the high sides. The bather washed while sitting in the tub. A sponge bath is washing the body in its entirety with a soapy sponge or cloth, using a container of water to rinse the sponge or cloth as the bather washed.

Bathtubs in the bath house were very basic. They were made of tin and plated with zinc, in a slightly elongated, oval shape, similar to today's bathtubs. Water was heated by the bucket full on the stove then poured into the tub, filling it to the desired

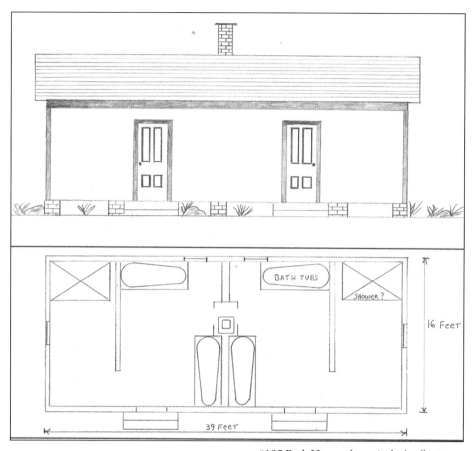

#105 Bath House plans. *Author's collection.*

#106 Tub. *Courtesy Mary Ann Fellner-Rapp*

#107 Sitz bath. *Author's collection.*

depth. It was not uncommon for more than one person to use the same bath water before it was bailed out. The areas on the blueprint marked with a draftsman's shower code are on each end of the building., a shower code is an "X" in a square. Showers were taken by having buckets of water poured into a vessel situated above the bather. The vessel had several holes in the bottom allowing the water to sprinkle onto the bather.

Commanding Officer's Quarters, "Custer House"- size: 52 feet by 80 feet

This two-story, frame structure, commonly referred to as Custer House, is the best known building in the fort, even though General Custer only lived in it three of the 18 years it stood. It was very opulent, considering what most fort housing was like. It had a parlor, bay window, music room, den/office, billiard room, dining room, kitchen, 3 bedrooms, a dressing room and a small basement for food storage. Outside there was a woodshed, garden enclosed by a high fence, wrap around porch, chicken coop, and privy.

The building seems to have numerous additions to it but it was mostly all built at one time. The first home was destroyed by fire on February 06, 1874, but rebuilt in the spring

#108 **Custer House.** *Author's collection.*

#109 Custer House. *Author's collection.*

#110 Custer House. *Author's collection.*

of 1875 with a bay window added to the original design. Years later the bay window was moved forward, and another room addition was constructed in its place.

In the photo, the rear of v can be distinguished by the white Sibley tent. It was given to him by his friend and foe, Tom Rosser. Rosser was a classmate of Custer's at West Point and a foe as a Confederate General during the Civil War. Even though they fought directly against each other in a few battles, they remained friends. The tent was a gift from Rosser who was directing the construction of the Northern Pacific Railroad through the Dakota Territory. In photo #4, Custer House has the Sibley tent behind it.

#111 Custer House. *Courtesy Little Big Horn Battlefield.*

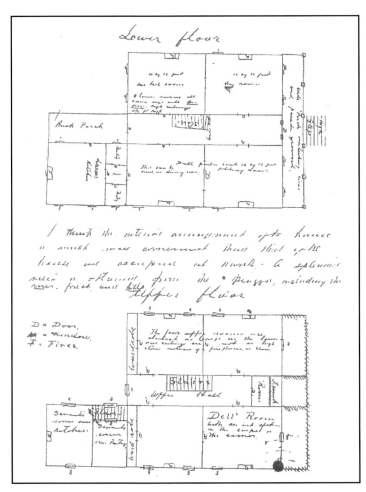

#112 Custer House floor plan. *Author's collection.*

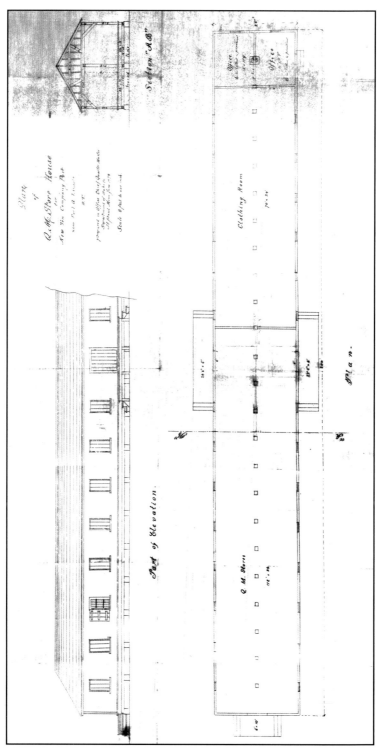

#113 Commissary blueprint. *Author's collection. Courtesy National Archives.*

#114 Commissary Store, Store Manager, "Sergeant" Lucy Dahner in the center, Dan Kautzman on the left and of course Fort Lincoln mascot, Daisy.
Author's collection. Courtesy Fort Lincoln Commissary Store.

Commissary- size: 25 feet by 200 feet

The building served the same purpose as the Infantry Post Commissary. The Cavalry commissary was 76 feet longer than the Infantry commissary. Today this reconstructed building houses the Gift Shop and meeting hall, with a small area as a replica commissary storage area.

#115 Commissary storage.
Author's collection. Courtesy Fort Lincoln Commissary Store.

Commissary Sergeant's Quarters- size: Unknown

The Commissary Sergeant was given his own quarters. It was a very small building but at least it was a private residence that he shared with no one.

In photo #5, the Commissary Sergeant's Quarters can be seen on the left side of the photo. It is the very small building to the left of the large, square N.C.O. Quarters.

Corral- size: unknown

The exact location of the corrals is unknown. It can only be assumed they were near the stables. The corrals were not used by the soldiers' horses, but rather, were to retain mules and old horses used by the Quartermaster for hauling wagons. By magnifying a few of the panoramic views of the cavalry post a huge square shape can be detected south of the stables. Upon further magnification there seems to be an opening in this square. Could this be a gate? Only man creates straight lines, and a square with four perfect right angles surely must narrow it down to a manmade object. Reference is made to the corral, yet no known photos exist.

In photo #3, at the extreme left center, a square fenced area appears with an opening like a gate. Could this be a corral?

Dead House- size: 16 feet by 16 feet

This dead house served the same purpose as the Infantry Post structure. Basic in design, it would only have one door and no windows. It was used to hold the dead until internment.

In photo #8, on the far left, directly behind the hospital, the Dead House may be visible. It appears to have a window, so it could be a Wood Shed instead.

Dispensary- size: 17 feet by 40 feet

The dispensary was used as the medical facility in lieu of having a hospital. It would be the equivalent of a clinic today. If more intense treatment were needed,

#116 Dead House site. *Author's collection.*

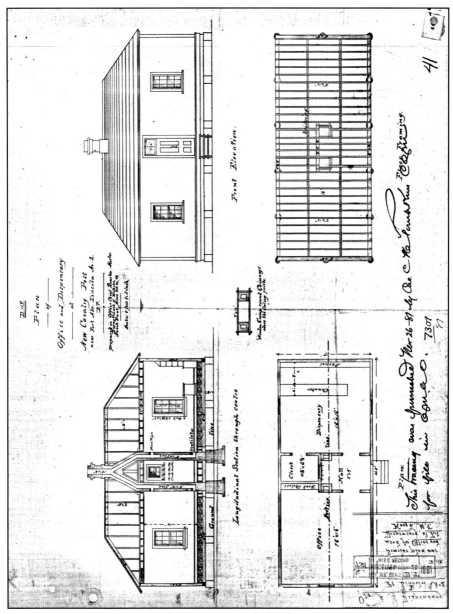

#117 Dispensary/Office blueprints. *Author's collection. Courtesy National Archives.*

the patient would be taken to the hospital. The dispensary is where the soldiers reported for sick call in the morning hours after roll call. Dispensary and hospital care was rudimentary to say the least. They were archaic compared to today's medicine. Back then, warming the feet was considered a cure for viral illnesses. We reflect upon this so called treatment and wonder how and why this could even be considered to cure an illness. A lot of our cures have been accidental and this warming of the feet may have been just that. Taking a hypothetical situation…

#118 Dispensary/Office site. *Author's collection.*

maybe a patient was being treated with warming of the feet and fully recovered. More than likely the patient may have recovered unassisted but this coincidence convinced the doctors that warming the feet was the reason for recovery and would continue prescribing this treatment for viral infections.

On the frontier, doctors would soon learn to give some type of credence to cures used by the Indians. An example being for decades the Indians had been using the ground up bark of the willow tree for curing headaches. The element in ground up willow bark that helped relieve headaches was "salicin," which is also used today in modern aspirins. Another item the Indians used was tobacco, to repel mosquitoes. At this point it must be addressed the misrepresentation surrounding the Indian "peace pipe." Smoking the peace pipe was not initially used to make peace with the white man. The Indians knew that tobacco repelled mosquitoes, and in hopes of repelling the white man, he offered the peace pipe to the white man in hopes that it would repel him as well.

#119 Granary. *Author's collection.*

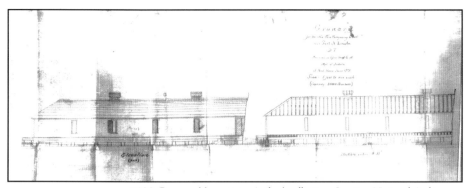

#120 Granary blueprints. *Author's collection. Courtesy National Archives.*

Granary- size: 25 feet by 200 feet

Granaries were used to store grains and forage for cavalry horses and Quartermaster's animals. The grain stored here was obtained through civil contractors.

Four small square structures project from the top of the granary. These structures are the ventilation system for the grain stored there. As grain sits and begins to decompose it becomes warm and begins to ferment, creating heat and gases. If those gases are not allowed to escape they become very volatile and create a danger from explosion that could be triggered with just static electricity.

These buildings have a historical significance also. During Custer's command at Fort Lincoln there were grain thefts, which prompted the fort to construct a dirt palisade on one side to prevent this theft. Custer discovered who the grain thieves were and took his troops into Bismarck to recover the stolen grain. This was totally out of his jurisdiction but that did not stop him. Custer was able to recover the grain with some of it being recovered from one of the storehouses owned by the mayor.

An often asked question arises: "Why not allow the horses to graze?" The answer... logistics. To allow over 600 horses to graze would be an unbelievable undertaking, requiring them to be moved further away from the stables as the grass became depleted.

Additionally, when an emergency required the rapid deployment of troops, it would be an impossibility to utilize horses that had to be chased down, lead back to the stables, saddled, and ridden to confront the emergency. This would almost negate the reason for having a cavalry for the deployment of troops. There would be horse losses through theft, wandering off, or predators. Also, a grain-fed horse is able to work much harder with longer stamina than one fed on grass. In the photo, the earthen berm built to deter grain theft can be seen in the foreground of the Granary.

#121 2nd Granary site. *Author's collection.*

#122 Guard House. *Author's collection.*

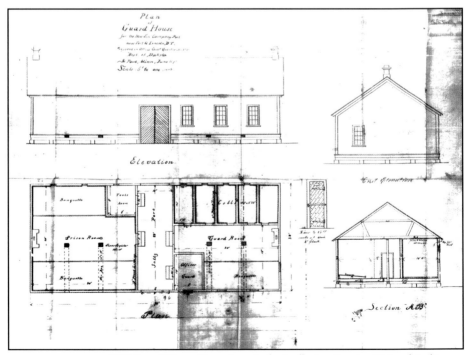

#123 Guard House blueprints. *Author's collection. Courtesy National Archives.*

#124 Guard House site. *Author's collection.*

Guardhouse- size: 30 feet by 72 feet

The guardhouse must be the most historic building in the entire fort. Granted, "Custer House" is the most well-known building, but only because Custer lived in it. Otherwise, it would be referred to as the Commanding Officer's Quarters. The blockhouses at the Infantry Post are well-known, due to using their images in books and advertisements. What is important about this building is that Chief Rain-in-the-Face, a Hunkpapa Sioux, was arrested by Tom Custer, the General's brother, for two murders committed during the Yellowstone Expedition in 1873. Rain-in-the-Face was incarcerated in this guardhouse awaiting a death sentence after being convicted of the murders. He was able to escape, possibly by design. Later, at the Little Big Horn Battle, Rain-in-the-Face reportedly cut out Tom Custer's heart and took a bite out of it.

This building is also of interest due to its huge side doors and security design. In the blueprints, the center area of the building is called a *"Sally Porte,"* which is Latin for "jump door" or "side door." *"Sally Port"* is a term used by current law enforcement agencies designating any police garage where squad cars are parked to load or unload prisoners. This term has been thought to have been a modern one. In past decades, police department *sally ports* have a drive-through design, with both doors being locked before loading or unloading prisoners. This guardhouse offers this same concept, but is ahead of modern police protocol by more than 130 years!

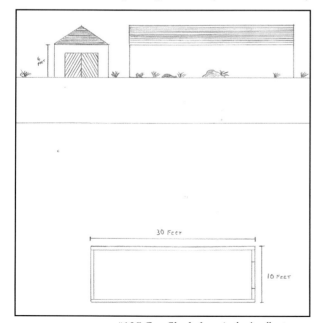
#125 Gun Shed plan. *Author's collection.*

Gun Shed- size: 10 feet by 30 feet

The gun shed at Fort Lincoln was four walls, a roof, and a door. It could have housed either cannons or small arms. At only 10 feet wide, it may have stored the cannons, but if a certain weapon were called for, the laborious task of moving other heavy weapons out of the way would have to be undertaken. If used for storing small arms, it would have been a large area for such storage.

#126 Hospital blueprint. Author's collection. *Courtesy National Archives.*

Hospital- size: 44 feet by 152 feet (wards and main building), 16 feet by 40 feet (kitchen area)

The hospital was similar in design to the Infantry Post Hospital. Besides battle wounds, the main maladies the hospitals addressed were scurvy, dysentery, diphtheria, typhus, cholera, and venereal diseases. A myriad of treatments were used to cure these maladies, but some had no effect what-so-ever or the treatment was worse than the illness. During the Civil War, wounded men would be laid under a tree. Since treatment for wounds was in its infancy, many wounded were left to die; the tree, therefore, was called the "dying tree." But many more soldiers died from disease than they did from battle. Fort Rice, in 1864, which was only 28 miles from where Fort Lincoln would be constructed, had a mortality rate of 75 deaths due to disease and 10 deaths due to battle.

Scurvy- (also called morphew)

Scurvy results from the lack of vitamin C, which is obtained through fruits and vegetables. *Symptoms:* Ashen colored skin, liver spots on the skin, spongy gums and bleeding from all mucous membranes. The victim shows depression and is partially, physically impaired. If left untreated suppurating wounds (pus covered) appear with the loss of teeth, then death.

Dysentery- (also called bloody flux or flux)

Dysentery results from the ingestion of water or food containing certain bacteria or from parasitic worms. *Symptoms:* Fever, cramping, painful passing of stool, diarrhea with blood in the stool.

Diphtheria- (also called putrid fever, sore throat distemper, or bullneck)

Diphtheria resulted from breathing the expelled air or by direct contact from a person infected by bacteria. It could have been obtained by infected cow's milk as well. It is highly contagious. *Symptoms:* Fever, sore throat with an adherent membrane on the tonsils, pharynx or the nose membranes.

Typhus- (also called hospital fever, spotted fever, or jail fever)

Typhus results from being bitten by a body louse infected with bacteria. *Symptoms:* Fever, rash, cough, headache, delirium, chills, muscle aches and sensitivity to light.

#127 Hospital site. *Author's collection.*

Cholera-

Cholera results from ingesting contaminated food or water. The bacteria may be more liquid related than food related. *Symptoms*: Fever, vomiting, cramps, and the skin may take on a bruised appearance, the eyes sink in and the lips turn blue. Major diarrhea results in dehydration then may cause death within hours.

Venereal Disease- (also called French Pox or Lues venera)

Mostly they had syphilis or gonorrhea. Venereal disease resulted from sexual contact with an infected person. *Symptoms*: Sores on the genitalia and if left untreated it may have an effect on the heart and brain. Treatment was with mercury, which in itself could cause kidney damage or mental illness. In photo #7, the Hospital is the two-story structure in the center of the photo. In photo #8, the Hospital is seen on the far left. In photo #9, the Hospital is senn on the far right. In photo #10, the Hopsital is located left center of the photo.

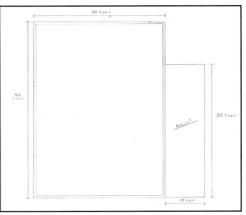

#128 Hospital Steward's Quarters.
Author's collection.

#129 Hospital Stewards site. *Author's collection.*

Hospital Steward's Quarters- size: 45 feet by 60 feet

The hospital was directed by the Hospital Steward. The steward was a non-commissioned officer with a thorough knowledge of English, writing, reading and math. They were in charge of all the bookkeeping and administrative duties. They were to have had practical knowledge of pharmacy to take care of the dispensary and also surgery. They were to be able to attend to wounds, apply bandages and pull teeth, as well as being able to cook meals for the patents. The steward was important enough to be given his own quarters when available.

The hospital steward was responsible for the hospital functions as well as the functions of the dispensary. The Hospital Steward and the surgeon were the only two men permanently attached to the medical department. The medical department also had its individual insignia, which is still in use today. The insignia is called a "Caduceus", with the actual design being a staff with wings on the top (representing the Greek messenger of the god's staff, Hermes, or the Roman messenger of the gods, Mercury) and two serpents entwined around the staff representing, knowledge and wisdom. On this insignia there may have been letters to designate the branch of service inside the medical staff such as "M" for Medical, "N" for Nurse and "V" for Veterinarian.

#130 Caduceus. *Author's collection.*

Ice House- size: approximately 48 feet by 48 feet

There was one Ice House at the cavalry post. In photo #8, the small square building above the right Barracks may be an Ice House. In photo #10, the building above the right Barracks may be the same Ice House as in photo #8.

Laundress' Quarters size: 30 feet by 180 feet

The Cavalry Post's laundress quarters were different from the Infantry Post's in two aspects. The Cavalry Post quarters were much larger, as it was capable of housing 24 laundresses. It was also built using a frame construction, as opposed to the log construction at the Infantry Post, which housed 16 laundresses.

Some laundresses may have been unmarried or married with children. Considering the time period, they were paid very well in comparison to a soldier's $13 a month. A laundress was paid $5 a month for doing an officer's clothing and $2 a month for doing an enlisted man's clothing. This may not seem like a lot initially but washing for four men earned the laundresses a considerable amount of money for a woman during that era.

Laundresses were private individuals given the right to do the laundry for the soldiers by the fort's commanding officer. They were highly sought after by soldiers for their income as well as other benefits of marriage. It became so difficult to keep single laundresses that the ladies requested the fort to hire only the most homely girls. Even that did not dissuade the desires of the soldiers. Some laundresses supplemented their income in other manners, such as baking pies, sewing, being a mid-wife, or selling female companionship.

Selling their companionship is where a common term "ladies-of-ilrepute" originated. During the Civil War, General Hooker allowed laundresses to travel along with his troops, as long as they lived on the outskirts of his camps, and this area became referred to as "suds row." Because General Hooker allowed these camp followers, even though headquarters frowned upon it, the women became known as "Hooker's Ladies," and then, of course, the term was shortened to "hookers." Laundresses were given quarters and rations as well as all the supplies needed to wash clothes, including tarps or tents to protect them from the elements as they washed clothes. In old photographs, suds rows can be readily identified by their white linens hanging out to dry.

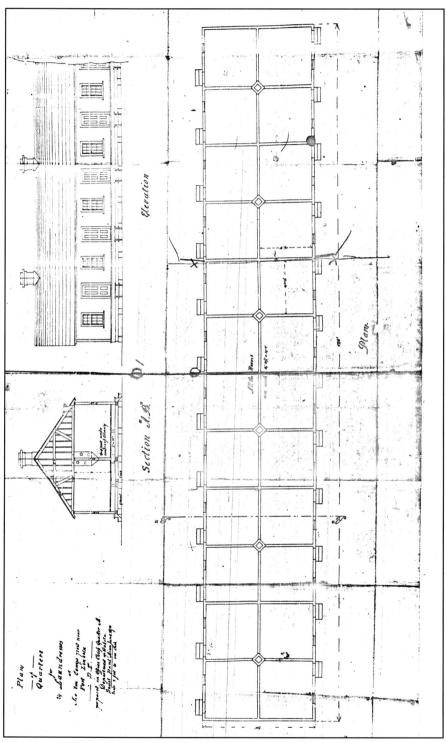

#131 Laundress Quarters blueprint. *Author's collection. Courtesy National Archives.*

Non-commissioned Officer's (N.C.O.) Quarters- size: 31 feet by 60 feet (barracks area); 8 feet by 18 feet (walkway); 18 feet by 40 feet (mess hall)

This building housed the remaining non-commissioned officers not living as 1st Sergeants in the enlisted men's barracks. In photos taken from a distance, it appears as though it was a two story, square building located next to the Band Quarters. The number of Sergeants billeted there is unknown. However, there is a difference in the building's shape at Cavalry Square and blueprints designed for the N.C.O. Quarters. The blueprints depict a structure similar in design and shape to the Band Quarters.

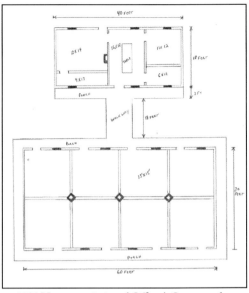

#132 Non-commissioned Officer's Quarters plan. *Author's collection.*

In photo #5, the N.C.O. Quarters is the large two-story, square building to the left of Barracks row and the Band Quarters. The shape of the building does not coincide with the blueprints.

Officer's Club- size: unknown

The Officer's Club was the entertainment hall for officers during off-duty hours. It must have had a billiard table, card tables, and of course alcohol. The building was off limits for Non-Commissioned Officers and enlisted men. It was reported that many of the officers in the military had alcohol problems, and with the construction of this building it can be assumed it made matters worse, since it made alcohol more readily available to them closer to Officer Row. Officers could drink to excess more often, since they were away from the enlisted men's eyes. Unlike common soldiers, who were severely punished for being drunk, an officer's drunkenness was overlooked as much as possible.

In photo #7, the Officer's Club is seen between the Granaries and Officer Row. In photo #8, the Officer's Club is the small, light colored building in front of the Granaries. In photo #10, the Officer's Club is the small, light colored building in the near center, in front of the two Granaries.

#133 Officer's Club site (where the dark brush is seen). *Author's collection.*

#134 Officer Row. *Courtesy State Historical Society of North Dakota, A2808.*

Officer's Quarters- size: 48 feet by 60 feet

The six Officer's Quarters were duplexes, making twelve residences. Unlike the

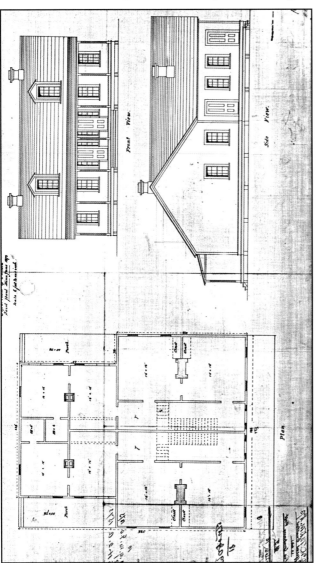

infantry post quarters, these were two stories tall and constructed with superior materials, such as plastered walls and ceilings. Still, their major downfall was the use of unseasoned cottonwood. With approval from the commanding officer, additions were constructed so that eventually none of the six buildings was alike. Each residence had a parlor, dining room, kitchen, two porches, and five bedrooms. Depending upon the "ranking out" procedures mentioned earlier, some of the buildings were designated as Officer Bachelor Quarters, for unmarried men or married men whose spouses were not at the fort.

#135 Officer Quarters blueprint. *Author's collection. Courtesy National Archives.*

#136 Officer Quarters sites. *Author's collection.*

Ordinance Depot-

Fort Lincoln was assigned an Ordinance Depot in 1878, consisting of seven buildings: an Officer's Quarters, barracks, carpenter shop, stable, depot building, storage building, and combination office/workshop. Located a considerable distance southwest of Cavalry Square, it was almost a separate post, as was the infantry post to the north. This depot was in charge of all weapons supplied at the fort, as well as their care and repairs. Anyone assigned to the ordnance department would not be transferred, since the ordnance belonged to the post. It was felt that enlisted men in the ordnance depot were more like ordinary citizens than soldiers.

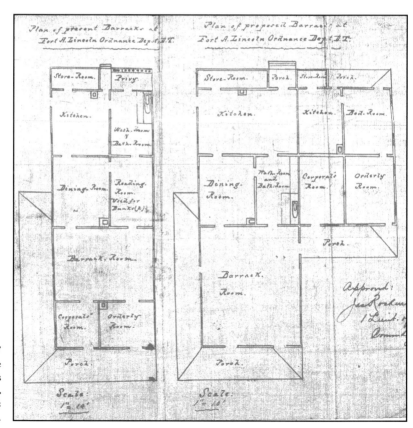

#137 Ordnance Barracks plans. *Author's collection.*

Ordnance Barracks- size: 24 feet by 76 feet, with an addition 24 feet by 45 feet

The Ordnance barracks were the living quarters for the enlisted men. They were much smaller and different in design than the barracks at the Infantry and Cavalry Posts. It had a barracks room, corporal's room, orderly room, kitchen, bathing room, dining room, reading room, store room, indoor privy, and wrap-around porch. Later, an addition housed the corporal and orderly with a private kitchen and bedroom. The original part of the building had the barracks enlarged and the reading room and privy removed.

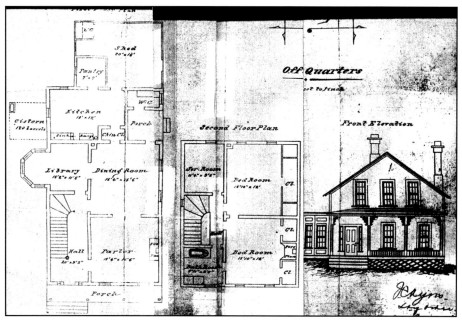

#138 Ordnance Officer Quarters plans. *Author's collection.*

Ordnance Officer's Quarters- size: 26 feet by 80 feet

The Officer Quarters for the Ordnance Department was much smaller than the Cavalry Post Quarters but were more elaborate in design. Its design was much more luxurious looking because of all the "gingerbread" cornices. It was a two story building with two bedrooms, a servant's room and bathing room upstairs. The main floor contained a parlor, dining room, library, kitchen, pantry, attached shed, cistern, indoor water closet, and porch.

Photo Studio- size: unknown

A photo studio at the fort had been approved by General Custer. It was constructed of available materials, according to Libby Custer. Whether that meant logs or frame construction is not known, but it is reported to have had a canvas roof.

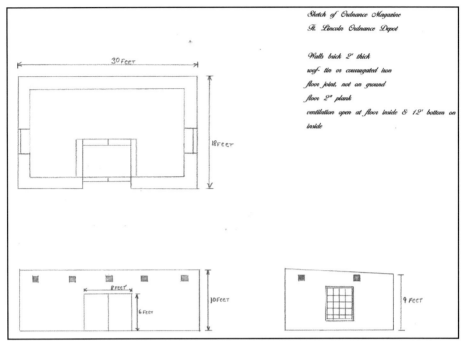

Sketch of Ordnance Magazine
Ft. Lincoln Ordnance Depot

Walls brick 2' thick
roof tin or corrugated iron
floor joint, not on ground
floor 2" plank
ventilation open at floor inside & 12' bottom on
inside

30 Feet

18 Feet

8 Feet

6 Feet

10 Feet

9 Feet

#139 Ordnance Powder House plan. *Author's collection.*

Powder House- size: 18 feet by 30 feet

The powder house, located southwest of Officer's Row, was built in an unusual location into a hillside for safety from explosions, but beyond protection from theft. Constructed during a time when attacks by Indians still occurred, it is hundreds of feet from the closest building at Cavalry Square and a thousand feet from the ordnance buildings. The blueprint of it is different than the powder

houses located at the Infantry Post. It is smaller and less detailed, and there seems to be no ventilation or drainage system. One wonders if this blueprint was a suggested design, or if it was meant for storage of lesser materials than those stored at the Infantry Post.

#140 Ordnance Powder House site (where the tree is located). *Author's collection.*

#141 Privy site behind Barracks. *Author's collection.*

Privy- size: 5 feet by 10 feet

Privies were all the same in design and shape throughout the fort. This photo shows the privy site behind the mess hall. The military tries to keep everything in a pattern, and the privy area was no exception. Nearby is a large indentation in the earth that may have been the "slop pit" for food scraps discarded by the kitchen.

Quartermaster Storehouse- size: 25 feet by 200 feet

This building served the same purpose as the Quartermaster storehouse at the Infantry post, but 76 feet longer.

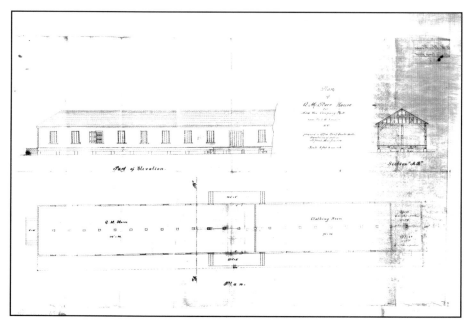

#142 Quartermaster Store House blueprint.
Author's collection. Courtesy National Archives

#143 Quartermaster Store House site. *Author's collection.*

Restaurant- size: unknown

The restaurant was a private business located on the Fort Meade Road, between the Cavalry Post and the Infantry Post. In photo #5, the Restaurant is believed to be the small building in the foreground. In photo #7, the Restaurant is believed to be the small building in the left foreground.

#144 Restaurant and unknown building site (where brush and tree are located). *Author's collection.*

Rifle Pits- size: various

Scattered quite a distance from the buildings are more rifle pits. When they were dug is unknown. They are located on privately owned land, so reseach is hampered.

Root Cellar- size: 25 feet by 40 feet

A root cellar was used to store vegetables, canned goods, or jars of "canned" jams, jellies, vegetables, or meat. It was constructed in a hillside and covered with dirt to take advantage of the earth's natural insulating abilities keeping things cool in the summer and

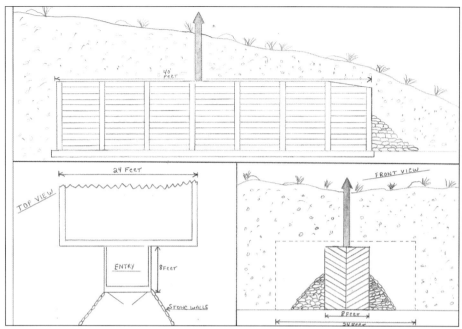

#145 Root Cellar plan. *Author's collection.*

#146 Root Cellar site (where tree is located).
Author's collection.

from freezing in the winter. This construction helped to prolong the storage of fruits and vegetables. Root cellars were vital in preventing scurvy, which plagued the 19th century soldier. In the early years out West, more soldiers died of scurvy than from combat.

Sawmill- size: unknown

The sawmill at the cavalry post was the old manual style probably used to make rough lumber used for wall supports, rafters, and ceiling joists. The more finished lumber, for floors, walls or siding, was made at the steam mill. The sawmill fell into disuse and was abandoned. The more efficient steam mill was located near the Infantry Post.

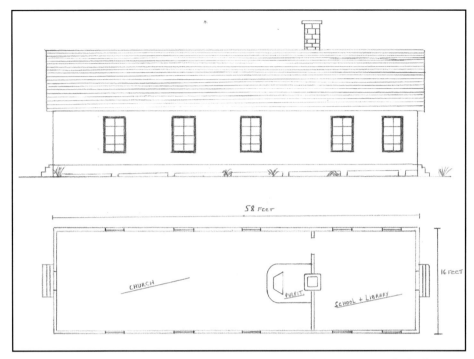

#147 School House/Chapel plan. *Author's collection.*

#148 School House/Chapel site (where bare spot is located). *Author's collection.*

School or Chapel- size: 16 feet by 58 feet

This structure was built for the dual purposes of serving as a schoolhouse and a chapel. The blueprints show that a majority of the space available was used as the chapel. It was common at forts for the officers' and enlisted men's children to have separate educational structures. Due to its location near Officer Row and the floor plan of a mere 16 foot by 16 foot area, this schoolroom was probably for the officer's children; there were fewer officers than enlisted men.

In photo #7, the School/Chapel is the long building on the far right. In photos #8 and #10, the School/Chapel is the light colored building in the right foreground.

Scout's Quarters- size: various

The Scout's Quarters were located south of the Laundress Quarters. They probably were constructed of logs. 45 scouts were assigned to Fort Lincoln; they did not wear uniforms and their horses and equipment were their own property.

A scout was responsible for locating good water, the best trails for travel, and adequate river crossings. He generally was a good hunter and helped provide food for the soldiers and was used to handle military dispatches. Scouts were able to track someone, using clues called "cutting signs." Although the clues may have been invisible to the common soldier, the signs spoke volumes to a trained scout. He knew that a bent piece of grass could reveal the direction of travel, the depth of horse tracks could determine if the horse was loaded or being ridden, and dry horse manure indicated how long it had been since the horse had passed there. The location of horse urine determined if it was a mare or a stallion, and that revealed a war party or women riders, since women rode mares. The warmth of ashes in a fire pit indicated how long the fire had been used. The horse's gait, or distance between hoof prints, indicated if the horses were running, walking fast, or taking it easy. If the horse had horseshoes, it was more likely owned by a white man. A scout knew that if hemlock trees were nearby, the top spire of the tree leans towards the east. Arrow fletching and design, fire pit design, and moccasin prints revealed the Indian tribe who made them.

If scouts were white men, they surely learned their trade from Indians. Red or white, he was expected to be familiar with the enemy's lifestyle and language and be able to communicate with them. Indian languages were interspersed with hand signs, most tribes using similar motions for certain words. Thus, tribes could interact with one another. General Custer was somewhat adept at this universal language.

In photos, #3 and #11, there are tepees barely visible on the left side of the photos. They are above and to the right of the center Barracks. This could be the location of the scouts' quarters, since it was explained that to enter Fort Lincoln, one had to pass through the Scout's Quarters area, then to the Laundress Quaretrs building. Do not confuse the white tents above the right Barracks; these are tents of visitng troops.

Stables- size: 30 feet by 212 feet

The stables housed 88 horses per building comfortably. Unlike the infantry post, these stables were of frame construction and were maintained by their own security system. It consisted of the Stable Guard, one Non-Commissioned Officer and two enlisted men, protecting the horses 24 hours a day to prevent the horses from running out. When the doors were open, a set of chains hung horizontally across the doorway, one chain set at 5 feet high and another at 2 1/2 feet high. These chains were connected by a vertical chain in the center, to prevent them from being tangled or pulled apart.[20] The majority of the stalls held two horses, with single stalls for ranking soldier's mounts. They were each equipped with feed bins and brackets to hold saddles, reins, blankets, and grooming supplies. At each end of the structure were two rooms. Speculation is that they were used by the Stable Guards.

When horses were placed out on picket ropes near the stables for grooming, armed guards constantly patrolled to prevent a horse from being stolen or accidentally become loose. Picket ropes were 100 feet long, with four posts supporting them, allowing 25 horses to be picketed between the posts. There were also Stable Police, who had nothing to do with security, they cleaned the stables. Today, the locations of two stables are cut through by a road and two other stable sites have become lost due to erosion by the Missouri River.

In photo #8, another Stable can be seen on the extreme right, above Officer Row. In the photo, the end door can be seen to be left open. In photo #10, the long building on the left above Officer Row is the Stable. This stable was built after one of the Stables in Cavalry Square burned down.

#149 Stable. *Author's collection.*

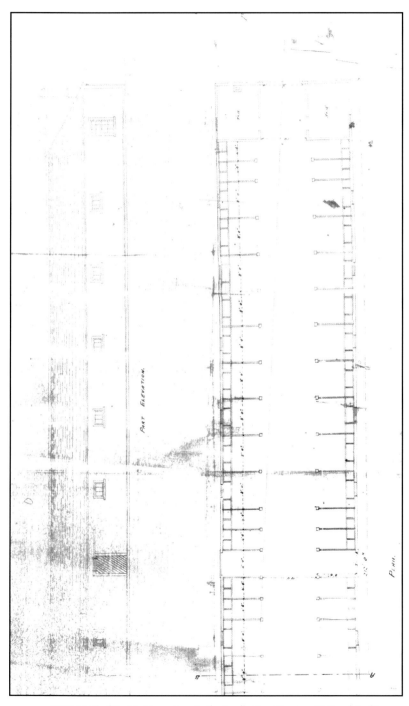

#150 Half of Stable blueprint. *Author's collection. Courtesy National Archives.*

#151 2nd Stable site. *Author's collection.*

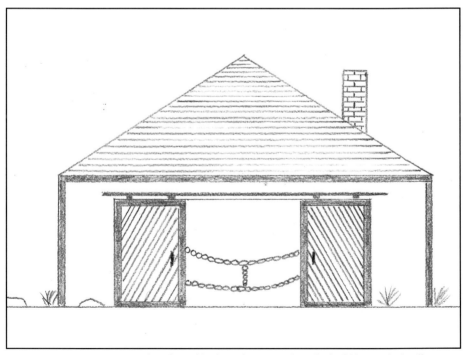

#152 What the stable door chains may have looked like. *Author's collection.*

#153 Stable picket rope. *Author's collection.*

#154 Stable stall. *Author's collection.*

#155 Custer, the thespian. *Courtesy Little Big Horn Battlefield.*

Theatre- size: unknown

The theatre was located south of the Workshop. General Custer gave approval for its construction for theatricals and dances at the fort. Made of available materials, it is uncertain today whether logs or framed construction was used. Actors who provided entertainment at the fort were from Bismarck or were soldiers trying their skill as thespians. Occasionally, the fort was visited by professional actors. General Custer was noted for his love of acting.

#156 Unknown building site by Granary.
Author's collection.

Unknown Buildings- size: A- unknown, B- unknown, C- unknown

Three unknown buildings stood around the Cavalry Post: a long one south of the Quartermaster Storehouse, a large one located north of the Granaries, and a small one between the Restaurant and Boarding House. Their functions are unclear, although research has been extensive. Two may have been wagon sheds and one may have been a wagon and carriage shed.

In photo #5, one of the unknown buildings is in the center of the photo. It is the tall, long building between the Granaries and the Restaurant. In photo # 6, the Unknown building can be seen in front of the Granaries.

Wood Shed- size: 20 feet by 40 feet

A blueprint discovered among the old files shows a Wood Shed, but the number built, location, and use are unknown. It stored wood, but was it lumber or firewood? It had two storage rooms with a door and a window in each. If firewood were stacked to the rafters, it would be capable of holding only 50 cords of wood. It seems unlikely that this was the purpose, unless it was for the Officers or Hospital, etc.

Work Shop- size: unknown

The purpose of the Work Shop can only be speculation, but it must have been used as a machine or tool shop for general repairs.

In photo #8, the Work Shop is the long building on the right, just above the Quarter Master Storehouse. The theatre was located to the

#157 Wood Shed plan. *Author's collection.*

south of the Work Shop. In photo #10, the Work Shop is located above the School or Chapel and Officer Row.

Chapter 4
Ordnance

#158 Caisson and Limber. *Courtesy Hal Jespersen.*

Ordnance at Fort Lincoln varied and the weapons shown here represent a small selection of those supplied to the soldiers. Smooth-bore weapons were less accurate than rifled armament, and those made of brass were stronger than those made of iron. Movement of the cannons was performed by horses, requiring six to pull the limber, cannon, and caisson. The limber was an ammunition chest on wheels that contained the shells, powder and fuses. It also provided a seat for the team driver and another artillerist. A caisson was a wheeled cart for two more ammunition chests and seating for four more artillerists; it carried a spare wheel and was used for the storage of ammunition and its supplies.

Heavy Weapons

#159 Napoleon cannon. *Courtesy Hal Jespersen.*

Weapon: 1861, 12-pound Napoleon Cannon
Bore: 4.62 inches
Bore type: Smooth bore
Material: Bronze
Barrel length: 66 inches
Barrel weight: 1,700 pounds
Range: 1,615 yards at 5 degrees
Ammunition: Solid shot, spherical shot, spherical case shot, canister, grape shot.
Information: Most common field piece in the Civil War. It fired a flat trajectory, rather than an arced trajectory and was used more for long-range conditions. It required 6 men to operate.

#160 Howitzer cannon. *Courtesy Hal Jespersen.*

Weapon: 1857, 12-pound Mountain Howitzer Cannon
Bore: 4.62 inches
Bore type: Smooth bore
Material: Bronze
Barrel length: 53 inches
Barrel weight: 788 pounds
Range: 1,072 yards at 5 degrees
Ammunition: Same as the Napoleon
Information: Used for short distances. It fired rounds in an arc like a mortar so the projectiles dropped behind enemy fortifications.

#161 3 inch Rodman Rifle. *Courtesy Hall Jespersen.*

Weapon: 3-inch Rodman Rifle
Bore: 3 inches
Bore type: Rifled
Material: Wrought iron
Barrel length: 69 inches
Barrel weight: 820 pounds
Range: 1,830 yards at 5 degrees
Ammunition: 3 inch Hotchkiss shell
Information: A Rodman rifle was a more accurate weapon than the other cannons due to the rifling inside the barrel. The rifling spun the projectile, stabilizing its flight and giving it more accuracy. It was the lightest artillery piece, yet the strongest. The rifled bore consisted of steel bands inside the barrel gradually twisting around toward the muzzle.

Weapon: Gatling Gun
Bore: .50 calibre and 1 inch. (100 calibers to an inch)
Material: Brass
Barrel length: 65 inches overall
Barrel weight: 90 pounds
Range: .50 caliber, 1 mile and the 1 inch, 2 miles.
Ammunition: Copper cased rim fire cartridges. .50 caliber fed at 200 rounds per minute and the 1 inch fed at 100 rounds per minute (30 cartridges per magazine).
Information: 6 Barrels hand-cranked like a meat grinder. It took four men to operate. The weapon was capable of swinging side to side for 60 degrees of coverage. (See photo #45)

Ammunition

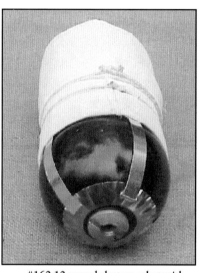

#162 12 pound shot on sabot with powder bag attached. *Courtesy AAA Munitions, Don Radcliff.*

Solid Shot: 12.3 pound solid ball with no explosive capabilities. It was used against fortifications but was deadly if used in a forest, as it shattered trees, sending thousands of lethal splinters flying about. It was also used against enemy artillery and wheeled equipment. Range was about 200 to 600 yards

Spherical Shot: A spherical shot was a hollow iron ball filled with an 8 ounce charge of black powder. It used a timed fuse to ignite the bursting charge. The shell exploded before reaching the enemy, throwing fractured pieces of the shell forward into enemy troops. It was also used to pierce wooden buildings and explode inside, spewing broken shell casing fragments throughout.

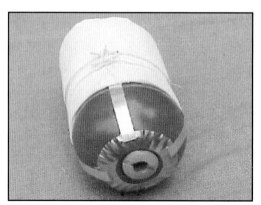

Spherical Case Shot: A spherical case shot was a hollow iron ball with thin walls filled with 84, .69 caliber balls or 78, .56 caliber balls suspended in sulphur using a timed fuse to ignite the sulphur. Used within 500 to 1,500

#163 12 pound spherical case shot.
Courtesy AAA Munitions, Don Radcliff.

#164 12 pound spherical case shot cut open to view interior
Courtesy AAA Munitions, Don Radcliff.

yards, it was designed to explode before reaching the enemy troops or explode above them. This ammunition was painted red for easy identification. The projectile was designed by an English artilleryman named Henry Shrapnel. This is where we get the term "shrapnel" for any flying piece of metal from an exploding projectile.

Canister: A canister was a large tin can filled with 27, 1.49 caliber balls stacked in 4 tiers that were packed in sawdust. The Mountain Howitzer cannon used 148, .69 caliber balls. Once fired, the tin canister disintegrated, sending the balls and broken tin can flying like a huge shotgun. Its effective range was 200 to 500 yards. Confederates also used ceramic balls instead of iron. This was not by design but rather was largely due to the lack of production of metal by the Confederacy. The ceramic balls were even more deadly though because they shattered into hundreds of razor sharp projectiles upon explosion.

Grapeshot: A grapeshot projectile was a large tin can filled with 9, 2.02 caliber balls stacked in three tiers held together with tin plates and a large iron bolt. When fired, this unit would break apart. It was used mostly by naval forces for destroying ship's rigging

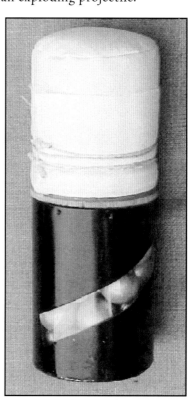

#165 Canister shot with see-through section to view interior.
Courtesy AAA Munitions, Don Radcliff.

and masts but in fact was also used by the army.

#166 Stand of grape shot. *Courtesy AAA Munitons, Don Radcliff.*

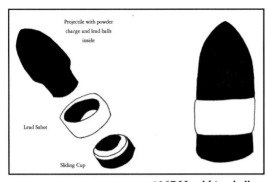

#167 Hotchkiss shell.

Hotchkiss Shell: The Hotchkiss shells were shaped more like a bullet. The case was hollow and filled with 16, ½ inch iron balls in black powder. On the outside of the base of the shell was a lead sabot surrounding it. Upon explosion of the propelling powder bag, a sliding pressure cup would be pushed forward compressing the lead sabot in length yet expanding it in diameter. This would cause the expanding lead sabot to "grab" hold of the rifling inside the barrel. As it moved forward through the barrel it caused the shell to spin thus giving it a more stable flight. The Hotchkiss shell used a timed fuse or percussion fuse.

Gatling Gun Ammunition: There were many various types of ammunition used by the Gatling guns. Research disclosed approximately 6 different types of ammunition so the sizes, both length and caliber, varied. The length varied up to almost 2 inches and the caliber varied almost .16 calibers.

#168 1 inch and .50 caliber Gatling Gun cartridge.
Courtesy Corbin's Mfg. And Supply, Inc., Dave Corbin

Wooden Sabot: "Sabot" is French for "shoe." All artillery shells had a sabot below the projectile or around it. A sabot could be made from wood or lead depending upon the type of projectile. Once the weapon was fired, the sabot separated from the projectile. Upon separation the sabot became part of the weapon as it flew toward the enemy either in one piece or shards of splinters. The sabots varied in shape and design but were used essentially as the medium used to connect the projectile to the powder bag or, in the case of the Hotchkiss shell, as the method for grabbing the rifling in the barrel of the cannon.

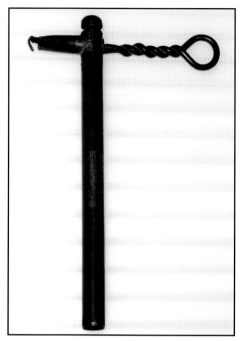

#169 Friction primer.
Courtesy Rock Island Arsenal.

Friction Primer: The device used to ignite the powder bag once it was placed inside the cannon was a friction primer. It consisted of a brass tube filled with powder and a friction composition. After loading the shot and powder bag into the cannon barrel, a wire was run down the vent hole of the cannon to pierce the powder bag. The friction primer was inserted into the vent hole. At a right angle near the top of the friction primer tube was a hole, with a serrated piece of brass wire running completely through it. The brass wire was attached to a long leather lanyard. When the gunner yanked on the lanyard it pulled the serrated brass wire through the brass tube and the friction compound caused a spark. The spark would ignite the powder in the brass tube, which in turn would ignite the powder bag.

Fuses

Fuses were set off by the explosion of the powder bag. The flame from the burning powder bag would ignite the powder fuse as it was propelled through the barrel.

Wooden Fuse: The first timed fuse was a tapered hollow piece of wood,

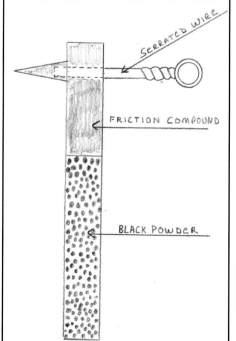

#170 Friction primer components.
Author's collection.

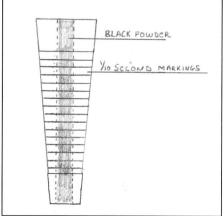

#171 Wood fuse.

similar to a long narrow funnel, which was packed with powder. The fuse was marked off in 10th of inches. For a shorter burn time, the fuse was cut to the required time needed.

Paper Fuse: Paper fuses were just that, paper rolled up with powder inside. They appeared like a tightly rolled piece of cardboard. A specified burn rate was tested on the lot of fuses then they were color coded to these burn rates. The rates were 10 seconds per inch, 7 seconds per inch and 5 seconds per inch.

Metal Fuse: This fuse was a small metal cup threaded so it could be screwed into the projectile fuse hole. The cup had a small channel packed with powder. This channel was protected by a very thin piece of tin marked off in seconds. To set the burn time, a hole was punched at the selected time needed, exposing the powder in the channel to the flames of the powder bag explosion.

Percussion Fuse: These were made to explode the projectile upon impact. This type of fuse used the inertia of the propelled projectile to ignite the fuse upon its sudden impact.

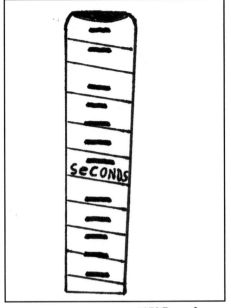

#172 **Paper fuse.**

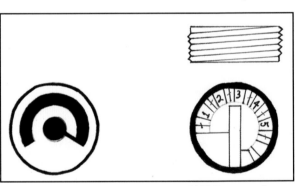

#173 **Bormann fuse.**

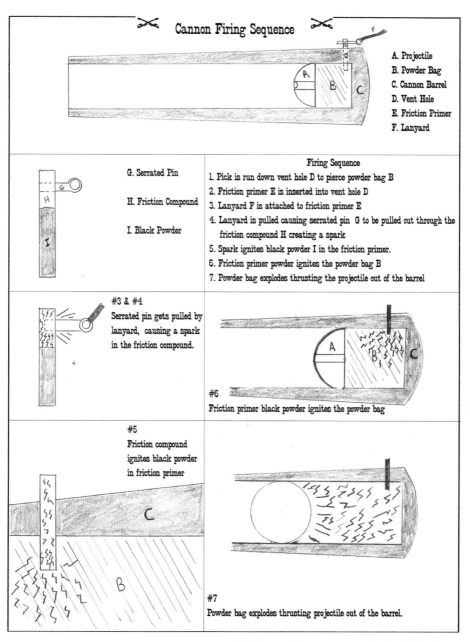

Cannon Firing Sequence

A. Projectile
B. Powder Bag
C. Cannon Barrel
D. Vent Hole
E. Friction Primer
F. Lanyard

G. Serrated Pin

H. Friction Compound

I. Black Powder

Firing Sequence
1. Pick is run down vent hole D to pierce powder bag B
2. Friction primer E is inserted into vent hole D
3. Lanyard F is attached to friction primer E
4. Lanyard is pulled causing serrated pin G to be pulled out through the friction compound H creating a spark
5. Spark ignites black powder I in the friction primer.
6. Friction primer powder ignites the powder bag B
7. Powder bag explodes thrusting the projectile out of the barrel

#3 & #4
Serrated pin gets pulled by lanyard, causing a spark in the friction compound.

#6
Friction primer black powder ignites the powder bag

#5
Friction compound ignites black powder in friction primer

#7
Powder bag explodes thrusting projectile out of the barrel.

#174 Cannon firing sequence. *Author's collection.*

Small Arms

Long Guns: These are better known as rifles. There were various types used by Fort Lincoln in the 19 years it was active. Throughout the lifetime of the fort, the rifle most often used was the 1873 Springfield. Before these were issued to Fort Lincoln in 1874, the soldiers carried the .50/70 caliber Spencer rifles and carbines. The Spencer had its benefits, such as firing 7 times before reloading due to a spring loaded tube that was inserted into the rear of the rifle. The two types of Springfield rifles used at Fort Lincoln from 1874 to 1891 were the rifle carried by the infantry and the carbine carried by the cavalry.

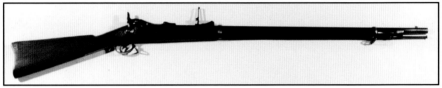

#175 1873 Springfield rifle (also referred to as a Trapdoor rifle). *Courtesy Rock Island Arsenal.*

Rifle: 1873 Springfield
Barrel length: 32.5 inches
Overall length: 52 inches
Weight: 10 pounds
Ammunition: 45/70, .45 caliber bullet with 70 grains of powder in the copper casing. (A grain of powder is .037 dram.)
Loading: It was loaded in a breech trapdoor with a single shot capability. The rifle was loaded by pulling back the chamber door (trap door) on top of the rifle. A cartridge (the bullet and the copper casing was inserted into the chamber then the trapdoor was closed. The rifle is also called the Trap Door Springfield due to this characteristic.
Range: 1,000 yards.

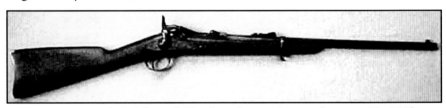

#176 1873 Springfield carbine. *Courtesy Antiquemilitari.com., Ken McPheeters.*

Carbine: 1873 Springfield
Barrel length: 22 inches
Overall length: 40 .5 inches
Weight: 7 pounds
Ammunition: .45/55 (.45 caliber bullet with 55 grains of powder in the copper casing)
Loading: Same as the rifle
Range: 400 yards

#177 **Loading an 1873 Springfield.** *Author's collection.*
Courtesy Fort Abraham Lincoln State Park Visitor's Center.

Handgun

Weapon: 1873 Colt .45 Single Action **Revolver**
Barrel length: 7 .5 inches
Overall length: 13 .250 inches
Weight: 2 pounds 13 ounces
Ammunition: .45 caliber copper cased center fire with 55 grains of powder.
Loading: 6 rounds in the cylinder. The thumb pulled back the hammer, revolving the cylinder and cocking the trigger at the same time.
Range: Sighted for 25 yards

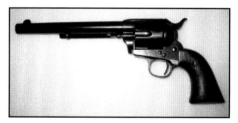

#178 **1873 Colt single action revolver.**
Courtesy Rock Island Arsenal.

Small Arms Ammunition

#179 **.45/70 cartridge (rifle).**
Author's collection. Courtesy Rock Island Arsenal.

Ammunition: .45/70 center fire copper casing
Cartridge: .45 calibers, 70 grains of powder in the copper casing with a center fire primer
Overall length: 2 .750 inches

Ammunition: .45/55 center fire copper casing
Cartridge: .45 calibers, 55 grains of powder in the copper casing with a center fire primer
Overall length: 2 .750 inches
Information: Both carbine and rifle cartridge bullets were seated the same depth so it was impossible to tell one from the other once they were removed from the cartridge boxes.

#180 .45/55 cartridge (carbine). *Courtesy Antiquemilitaria.com, Ken McPheeters.*

#181 .45 cartridge (revolver). *Courtesy Antiquemilitaria.com, Ken McPheeters.*

Ammunition: .45 caliber Colt center fire copper casing
Cartridge: .45 calibers with 30 grains of powder
Overall length: 1 .5 inches

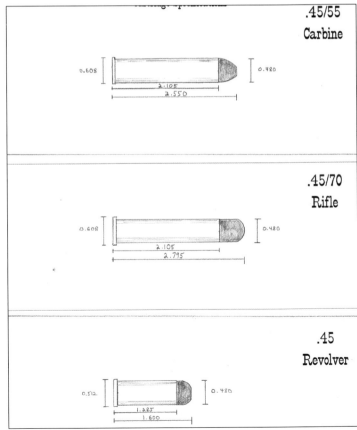

#182 .45/70, .45/55, .45 cartridge specifications. *Author's collection.*

Edged Weapons

Edged weapons, commonly called knives or swords, have been involved in warfare since time immortal. At Fort Lincoln the cavalry soldiers were issued sabers, but it soon became apparent that a saber was a useless weapon in Indian warfare because of the Indian's style of combat. It was often left behind on campaigns against the Indians but was still retained for use during Parade Dress.

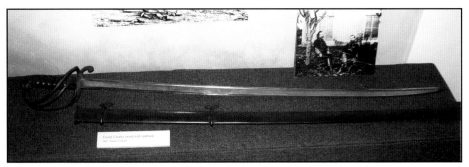

#183 Custer's cavalry saber. Author's collection. *Courtesy Monroe County Museum.*

Sabers
Weapon: Light Cavalry Saber
Overall length: 42.35 inches
Weight: 3 pounds 7 oz.

Knives
Almost every soldier carried a knife of some kind. The variety of knives varied according to one's imagination. Many were factory manufactured, but others were home-made. They varied in size, style, shape, and use. Some home-made knives could have been made from a sharpened flat piece of steel or file. The handle could have been fabricated from two pieces of wood or even a deer's antler. A few were over 18 inches long or they could be a simple, folding jack-knife.

During this era there were a couple unique knives manufactured and distributed among the troops. They are mentioned primarily because of their diverse style. They *may* have been carried and used by the soldier's at Fort Lincoln, or at least owned by a few.

Bowie Knife
Another large knife that may have been owned by soldiers at Fort Lincoln was the famous Bowie knife. One legend has it that Jim Bowie made his first knife from a meteorite he had recovered, after watching it plummet to earth. A true Bowie knife had a distinctly shaped blade. The tip of the blade had a slight upward curve and was sharp on both sides. Besides having the hilt protecting the hand, there was a brass plate going down the blade for about 8 inches on the upward curved side of the knife. This brass bar was designed to block an

#184 Custer's Bowie type knife. *Author's collection. Courtesy Monroe County Museum*

opponents slashing movement. The proper way to hold a true Bowie Knife seemed awkward since it was held with the long side of the blade upward. The reason being, after blocking an opponent's knife with the blocking bar, the Bowie knife would be thrust into the opponent then pulled upward, eviscerating them. As the Bowie knife gained notoriety, it soon became accepted to call any heavy long bladed knife a Bowie knife. General Custer also owned a Bowie style knife.

Weapon: Bowie knife
Blade length: Varied from 6 inches to 12 inches
Blade width: Varied from 1 .5 inches to 2 inches
Blade thickness: .250 inch
Overall length: 11 to 19 inches

D-Guard Knife

The D-Guard knife is included because the Civil War wast over for only a few years and some of the soldiers may have taken their knives with them to continue their military life. This knife was manufactured by the Confederacy for its soldiers during the Civil War. It resembles a short heavy sword with a "D" shaped guard protecting the hand. If a soldier was not issued this weapon, it could be made rather easily from a broken long sword. It only required the broken blade to be sharpened and honed to a desired length and shape. General Custer in fact owned one of these knives. It was presented to him by Company A of the 4th Michigan Infantry after they captured it from the Louisiana Tigers at the Peninsula Campaign of the Chickahominey.

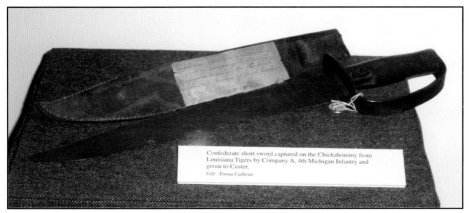

#185 Custer's D-guard type knife. Author's collection. *Courtesy Monroe County Museum.*

Weapon: D-Guard knife
Blade length: 19 inches
Blade width: 1.625 inches
Blade thickness: .1875 inch
Weight: 1 pound 5 ounces
Overall length: 23 inches

1881 Hunting Knife

The Model 1881 Hunting Knife was produced and issued specifically for the Indian Wars as the first general purpose knife adopted by the U.S. Army since before the Civil War. It was realized that the bayonet was a useless combat weapon during these wars and that the Hagner Entrenching Tool was inadequately designed for its purposes. However, it was noted that a special tool might be needed on the plains.

The hunting knife had two basic uses in its design. The first, as an entrenching tool and the second, as a knife to butcher game while out on campaign. This knife was not used like the Hagner Entrenching Tool since it didn't mount on the end of a rifle. This tool used good old hand power to dig into the earth. Of course there was a third use for this

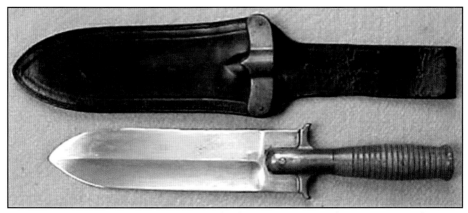

#186 1881 Hunting knife. *Courtesy Antiguemilitari.com, Ken McPheeters.*

knife. That being what all knives can be used for in combat. In a last ditch effort of hand to hand combat a knife as sturdily built as this could be a nice edge (pun intended).

This knife looks similar to the Hagner but its blade is only two inches wide. The knife itself was manufactured at the National Armory in Springfield, Massachusetts with the leather sheaths being manufactured at the Rock Island or Watervliet Arsenals.

Weapon: 1881 Hunting Knife
Blade length: 8.250 inches
Blade width: 2 inches
Overall length: 14.625 inches

Hospital Steward's Knife

Issued in 1888 for the Indian and Spanish American Wars this knife may have been carried by the Fort's Hospital Steward. It was in fact designed more as a tool than a weapon. It was issued to Hospital Stewards so they could hack away at underbrush to make clearings for patients or to cut wood for litters or shelter poles. Of course, in a last ditch effort it could become a formidable weapon.

#187 1888 Hospital Steward's knife. *Courtesy Rock Island Arsenal.*

Weapon: **Hospital Steward's Knife**
Blade length: 12 .250 inches
Overall length: 17 .750 inches long

Entrenching Tool

Another edged weapon carried by the troops at Fort Lincoln was called an "entrenching tool." It was used as a knife, bayonet, and shovel. The entrenching tool was an interesting item but had its downfall when being used as a bayonet. For example, charging enemy lines was a tactic of the past, especially during the Indian Wars. As a shovel, it fell short of its intended use when mounted on a rifle. Using it to dig created two problems: when shoved into the earth and pried back to break up the dirt, firm dirt made it bend the barrel of the rifle, making the rifle useless since a bullet could not exit the muzzle. Pressure from gases in the barrel built up in the rifle causing the rifle to explode, harming or killing its owner. In appearance, the entrenching tool reminds one of a hand-held garden spade or a small mortar blade. The tool shown is a Model 1873 Hagner Entrenching Tool, manufactured at the Rock Island Arsenal in Rock Island, Illinois. The soldier who owned this tool was J. Kelly, Company I of the 7th Cavalry.

Weapon: 1873 Hagner
Entrenching Tool
Blade length: 8 .250 inches
Blade width: 3 .5 inches
Overall length: 14 .625 inches

#188 1873 Hagner Entrenching tool. *Courtesy Antiquemilitaria.com. Ken McPheeters.*

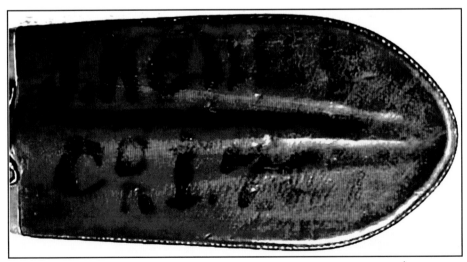

#189 Entrenching tool sheath, once owned by J. Kelley, Co. I. 7th Cavalry.,
Courtesy Antiquemilitaria.com, Ken McPheeters.

1873 Springfield Bayonet

The days of charging a mass of men (as was done in the American Civil War) had passed, so there was little use for a bayonet. When battling in close quarters with Indians, fighting with a knife, bare handed, or swinging rifle butts was more likely. With the exception of an occasional battle, bayonets used during the Civil War were more often used to hold meat or a pan over a campfire or as a stake of some sort. The bayonet was triangular in shape for a specific purpose; even with today's technology a triangular wound is difficult to treat. The bayonet could also be considered a biological weapon because when mounted to the rifle barrel, the bayonet was offset to allow the bullet to be fired fro the barrel. Then, black, sooty, burned gunpowder covered the bayonet and when thrust into a body it could inflict a mortal wound, even in an arm or leg. If not an immediate death, the bayonet could kill the victim by infection or cause a limb to be amputated.

Weapon: 1873 Springfield Bayonet
Design: Triangular shaped blade
Length: 18 inches

#190 1873 Springfield Bayonet.
Courtesy Rock Island Arsenal.

Chapter 5
People and Things

General George Custer

What can possibly be said about General Custer that hasn't already been placed on paper? Of course, this book is a new slant. Custer seemed to be an individual who was liked or loathed, with no middle opinion. He was accused of being an uncaring tyrant, yet his soldiers followed him into battle without hesitation. Custer led his men into battle regardless of his rank. Many generals have been despised because of aggressive battle tactics, for example General U. S. Grant who had high mortality rates among his soldiers, yet was successful in winning battles. With Custer, his energy was eternal and he could stay in the saddle for hours, leading him to receive the sobriquet, "hard ass." He could ride all day and, as his men bedded down for night, write letters to his wife for hours, some running to 80 pages long.

General Custer cared for his men, but in a way most people don't recognize as concern. One must have military or paramilitary background to understand that Custer was a stickler for training and discipline among his soldiers. Most forts did not have firearms training for months or maybe years. But the 7th at one time was required to fire their weapons twice a week to be prepared for battle. Custer was not satisfied with his troopers standing, kneeling, or lying down while shooting holes in targets. He also made them practice by firing their weapons while mounted on horseback. At this time in history, firearms practice was paid for by the officer ordering practice. Therefore, some soldiers never had the opportunity to fire their weapons before actual battle. Some forts lacked in parade drills and equestrian skills. Not so with Custer. He required his troopers to perfect their riding skills, and cared enough of them to require the skills needed for survival in combat. This attitude was leaps and bounds ahead of other commanders of that time.

After the Civil War, General Custer's every action was scrutinized by the public. For example, one major incident *may have* had tragic ramifications upon him later at the Little Big Horn. In the Washita Battle, General Custer left a missing contingent of 19 troopers under the leadership of Major Elliot. The last anyone saw of this force was as it charged over the hills, chasing a group of fleeing Indians. As Custer supervised the details of destroying Indian supplies and ponies, and handling dead, wounded, and captured Indians, as his orders commanded, he received information about another Indian village downriver, that some said was ten times bigger than the village they had just captured. The larger village was in the same direction that Major Elliot and his men had charged. Custer had a dilemma. Should he attack a larger encampment with fewer troopers to support his valiant major? Or, should he continue to supervise dead and wounded troopers and guard the captives, thus depleting his initial attacking force. To add to his quandary, his troopers had just made a forced march through a snow storm with twelve to eighteen inches of snow in below-zero temperatures and spent a grueling, miserable night without blankets and fires to avoid detection while awaiting an attack at daylight. Custer's forces were taxed physically and mentally, and low on ammunition. To launch an attack on a much superior force could have been disastrous. It might have been Custer's Last Stand, but eight years earlier and in Oklahoma, instead of Montana.

With leadership comes responsibility and some overwhelming decisions. Was Custer to follow Elliot and risk losing his entire command, or should he escort his beleaguered forces back to safety, food, and warmth? Custer may have thought Elliot would break off the chase and return to the 7th's protection. Elliot knew he was going into a very perilous situation since he had asked for volunteers. Elliot had made the heroic statement, "Here's for a brevet or a coffin," and charged off after his prey.

Research by military tacticians has since concluded that with the conditions Custer faced, he made the proper decision to break off the engagement and return to base for the safety of everyone. This decision would haunt him, because he lost the trust of most his officers and troopers; Major Elliot was well liked and a respected officer. It was thought that if Custer would "desert" a trusted officer like Elliot, he wouldn't hesitate to leave them, too, should they become cut off from the main force.

But Custer's superiors must have concurred with his actions. Only a few months earlier, Colonel Sully, while out on campaign, had left behind two soldiers who were seen being abducted by Indians; he continued on with his march instead of going back to help them. Sully was castigated by Sheridan, and the incident may have been the reason Custer was offered command of the 7th. Yet Custer was accused of deserting 20 men and he did not receive even a verbal reprimand. If Custer had acted inappropriately, his commanders would not have hesitated to profer charges. As proof, almost a year prior to Washita, they filed charges against the Civil War hero for offenses less dramatic than his orders to disengage hostile forces at Washita.

Could scathing letters to the press and the loss of trust in Custer by his subordinates be *part* of the reason Custer continued his attack at the Little Big Horn? The worst thing a soldier can say about another officer or soldier is that they can't be relied upon for support when a dangerous situation arises.

At the Little Big Horn, as far as Custer knew, Major Reno was in a heated battle in the valley, after he had told Reno he would support him. Custer also thought that Benteen (Custer's biggest detractor) would be following his orders and would be pulled into the battle also. Did Custer, after realizing the village was too large and that he had men in combat to support, decide to charge into the village to prevent being accused of not supporting an arm of his command... again?

#191 General Custer (Bloody Knife kneeling on Custer's right).
Courtesy Little Big Horn Battlefield.

Bloody Knife

Bloody Knife was General Custer's favorite scout and a half-breed Arikara and Hunkpapa Sioux. While growing up, Bloody Knife had a harsh life; he was beaten and denigrated by the Sioux because of his mixed blood. However, he was more fortunate than his two brothers, who had been killed by Chief Gall of the Sioux. Bloody Knife had the opportunity to wreak revenge upon Chief Gall when Gall had been beaten in a fight. Bloody Knife was about to take out his rage on Gall, but was stopped by other tribe members. Chief Gall was wounded and unconscious, but after he was treated he fully recovered. This incident had devastating ramifications later, at the Little Big Horn.

Bloody Knife was Custer's scout during the Yellowstone expedition, the Black Hills expedition, and the tragic Little Big Horn campaign. Before the Little Big Horn battle, Bloody Knife had warned Custer that there were too many Indians to fight. Custer didn't heed this advice, but tried to convince Bloody Knife to avoid the fight. Possibly, Custer knew the hatred the Sioux had for Bloody Knife, and that, if captured, Bloody Knife would be tortured. Bloody Knife became attached to Major Reno's command in the valley. When Bloody Knife was shot in the head during Reno's attack, retreat, and rout, his cranial blood splattered over Major Reno. This may have contributed to the reason Reno reportedly panicked and gave countermanding orders. When the Sioux discovered the body of their much-hated kin, they decapitated him, amid other disfigurements, and thrust the head upon a pole for display in the village.

Tom Custer

Thomas Ward Custer, the younger brother of General George Custer, deserves special recognition. If Tom had lived longer, he may have attained his own General's star. Though guided and aided by his famous brother, he was not given preferential treatment from General Custer. In fact, General Custer made things more difficult for Tom in order to show others that he was not giving his brother special treatment.

Tom Custer's fame, unfortunately, will forever be connected to the defeat of the 7th Cavalry at the Little Big Horn. He was an energetic and brave man whose personal claim to fame is that he was the only *soldier* to win the United States' most prestigious award, the Congressional Medal of Honor, twice during the Civil War. As a Second Lieutenant, he earned his first Medal of Honor on April 03, 1865 at Namozine Church, Virginia, by charging Confederate lines and seizing the battle flag of the 2nd North Carolina Cavalry. Capturing an enemy's battle flag was one of the most disruptive acts that could be done in battle, because it disorganized and demoralized the enemy troops. On April 06, 1865, just three days after capturing the first flag, Tom charged enemy lines at Saylers Creek, Virginia, leaped over Confederate breast works, and captured a second battle flag. For that he earned a second Medal of Honor, but paid a terrifying price for it. As he grasped the standard pole and jerked it free from the color bearer's control, Tom was shot in the face. Fortunately, the bullet went through his cheek and exited behind his jaw. Tom was able to maintain control of the flag and he returned with his coveted prize to the safety of his own troops. After

#192 Tom Custer. *Courtesy State Historical Sotciety of North Dakota, 0022H0025*

depositing the flag into safe hands, Tom attempted to return to battle, even though he was wounded. Upon seeing Tom's wounds and his attempt to get back into the fight, General Custer had Tom arrested and escorted to the rear to have his wounds treated. Tom was the only soldier to win the two Medals of Honor for two separate actions, making him the highest decorated soldier in the Civil War. There have been only 19 other men to receive this medal more than once, in the entire history of the United States.

Brave, loyal, admired, and respected, Tom was all boy at heart. One of his favorite pastimes was capturing and playing with rattlesnakes out West. It was not an uncommon sight to see Tom with a bag full of rattlesnakes tied to his saddle. He was also an avid prankster, who loved to pull jokes on his friends and family. In Tom's honor, the next building to be reconstructed at Fort Lincoln will be Tom's Quarters.

Grant Marsh

Grant Prince Marsh was perhaps the greatest riverboat captain ever. As a First Mate aboard the boat *A. B. Chambers 2*, Marsh also served aboard the *A. B. Chambers 1*, he served with a Second Mate by the name of Samuel Clemens, better known as author Mark Twain. Asked to recall Grant Marsh, Twain gave the highest praise possible of his former shipmate.

Marsh's abilities became apparent after he signed on with the Coulson Packet Lines in Yankton. He piloted the *Nile*, the first steamboat to stay the winter on the upper Missouri River, and again the following winter on the *North Alabama*. These voluntary winter trips were necessary for new forts that required supplies for the winter. Marsh was no stranger to service with the military. During the Civil War he worked for the United States fleet on the lower Mississippi River.

Due to Marsh's familiarity with military protocol, he was chosen to explore the Yellowstone River. In 1873, while piloting the *Key West*, he went 460 miles upriver. In 1875 he set a record piloting the *Josephine* 483 miles upriver, a record never to be accomplished again by a steamboat. Marsh was chosen by the military for three historic events. His ships were used as the supply vessels for Custer's Yellowstone Expedition, the supply/mobile headquarters/hospital ship for the Little Big Horn Campaign, and as the ship that transported Sitting Bull and his tribal members from Fort Yates to Fort Randall to be incarcerated.

After piloting 22 steamboats in his career and placing his name in the history books, he was relegated to towing barges of cement, coal, and grains up and down the Missouri River. He died a pauper and is buried at Bismarck's St. Mary's Cemetery, overlooking the Missouri River.

Mitch Bouyer

Mitch Bouyer was a half-breed Santee Sioux on his mother's side and a Frenchman on his father's side. He and one of his brothers met infamous, untimely deaths. His brother was hanged in Wyoming for killing an Army Scout. (His death was the first legal execution in Wyoming.) Mitch was killed at the Battle of the Little Big Horn.

Tutored by the famous scout, Jim Bridger, Mitch became a scout for the 2nd U.S. Cavalry as a civilian, until Custer requested Mitch's transfer to the 7th Cavalry. Mitch became such a nemesis to the Sioux as a scout that Sitting Bull offered a reward of 100 ponies for Mitch's death.

Bouyer was one of the scouts who warned Custer not to attack the overwhelming hoard of Indians at the Little Big Horn. During an archaeological examination of the surrounding terrain at the battlefield, a cheekbone was discovered with Mongolian/Caucasian characteristics. Mitch Bouyer was the only one who met that racial mix at the battle. Through modern technology, a photograph of Mitch Bouyer was superimposed over the cheek bone fragment, verifying without a doubt that it was the loyal scout's cheekbone.

Isaiah Dorman

Isaiah Dorman was a Negro scout for the 7th Cavalry. Mostly assigned to Fort Rice, Dorman would occasionally be at Fort Lincoln. Little is known about Isaiah, except for bits of information here and there. Thought to have been an escaped slave from Texas or Louisiana, nothing prior to his arrival around the Bismarck area is known for sure. He was a woodcutter for steamboats along the Missouri River, for the trading post of Durfee & Peck, as well as for Fort Rice.

Later he married a Santee Sioux woman, who was the God-daughter of Chief Sitting Bull. He was called two different names by the Sioux: *Azinpi* and *Wasisun Sapa*. *Azinpi* closely resembled the way the Sioux pronounced Isaiah, so they called him *Azinpi* instead, which meant buffalo teat or teat. *Wasisun Sapa* translated into black, white man. He was called Buffalo Teat, but it had nothing to do with the reverence the Indians had with the buffalo. A common misconception with today's society concerns the reasons Negros were called buffalo men or buffalo soldiers. It is not entirely due to the Indians respecting the gallantry of the Negros, but rather something less romantic. The reason was two physical similarities the Indians saw between the buffalo and the *wasisun sapa*. The first was that their skins were both black, and the second was that their curly hair resembled each another.

Dorman became adept at the Siouan language and eventually became an interpreter, then a scout. Most of his interpretive skills were for the Northern Pacific Railroad crews constructing the track through Dakota Territory. Dorman seemed to be a man of all trades, since he also delivered the mail between Fort Rice and Fort Wadsworth (also known as Fort Sisseton). He may have been used as a scout for the Black Hills Expedition with Custer. Requested as a scout for the Little Big Horn campaign, Dorman met his death in the valley fighting with Major Reno's detachment.

It was reported that Isaiah's horse was shot and as it fell Isaiah became pinned under the dead horse. Some say Chief Sitting Bull recognized *Wasisun Sapa* and ordered that no harm was to come to the husband of his God-daughter. Sitting Bull gave Dorman a drink of water then continued on. Once Sitting Bull was gone, the women began attacking Dorman with stone mallets, crushing his skull. They severed his penis and stuffed it into his mouth, then drove a picket pin (a steel spike used to tether a horse) through his testicles. He was slashed with knives, the common practice to fallen enemies. The harsh treatment must have been because he was considered a member of the tribe who turned traitor, just as Bloody Knife had been decapitated, then displayed.

Lonesome Charlie

Charles Alexander Reynolds became a scout for the 7th Cavalry at Fort Lincoln along with 44 others. He was known as Lonesome Charlie because of his wandering ways and his propensity to keep to himself. Because of his silence concerning his private life, little is known about him. Born in Illinois, the son of a doctor, Charley tried extending his education by attending college, but soon dropped out. When the Civil War erupted, Charlie's loyalty stayed with the Union and he joined the infantry. After the war, Reynolds became a buffalo hunter and scout. His hunting skills were so good the Indians named him White-Hunter-Who-Never-Goes-Out-For-Nothing.

Lonesome Charlie was known to read whenever he could obtain a book. He must have been elated as a scout on the Yellowstone and Black Hills Expeditions. Taken along on the expeditions were numerous scientists specializing in various fields. Reynolds would finally have someone to talk to about his favorite subject, geology.

Lonesome Charlie met his death at the Little Big Horn. He knew he wouldn't survive the day. Reynolds was assigned to Reno's Command. Atop "Reno's Hill." Lonesome Charlie saw that the Indians were trying to shoot the doctor who was treating a wounded soldier. Charlie yelled at the surgeon, gaining his attention. As Charlie tried to go to the doctor's aid, Charlie was shot and killed. The doctor survived the siege because of Lonesome Charlie's actions.

Chief Rain-in-the-face

Rain-in-the-face, *Ito-na-gaju*, was a controversial person concerning Fort Abraham Lincoln and the Custer Clan. He was a well-noted Lakota war chief of the Hunkpapa Sioux. Such an unusual name was acquired by two separate episodes. The first incident was when Rain-in-the-face was a young boy. He got into a fight with an older boy, and when the fight was over Rain-in-the-face stood with splattered blood dripping down his face, appearing as if it were rain drops. The second incident was during a battle with another Indian tribe. After the fight, Rain-in-the-face's white and black war paint had streaked, and again it appeared as though it was rain droplets on his face.

Rain-in-the-face was a true warrior and he loved battle. He was involved in five well-known battles with white men. One was at Fort Totten, in the northeast corner of present-day North Dakota. Another was at the Fetterman "Massacre." The third was during the Yellowstone Expedition. The fourth was at the Battle of the Rosebud. The fifth was the Battle of the Little Big Horn.

Kismet entered into Rain-in-the-face's life with the Custers during the Yellowstone Expedition. Dr. Honsinger, the veterinary doctor, and Post Sutler Baliran had been repeatedly warned not to wander off but to stay within the protection of the main forces. They chose to go off on their own in search of gold, and it cost them their lives. The crime was unsolved for nearly a year when several Indians at the Standing Rock Reservation overheard Rain-in-the-face bragging about his gruesome murders of the doctor and the sutler. Upon hearing that Rain-in-the-face was in hiding at the Standing Rock Reservation, Captain Tom Custer was ordered to travel to the reservation and arrest Rain-in-the-face.

It was reported that Tom Custer beat Rain-in-the-face during the arrest, but it was also reported that it was just a slap. However, most men would rather be hit with a fist and knocked down or knocked out than to be slapped, especially a proud warrior like Rain-in-the-face. A slap would have been considered a great insult to the warrior. Whether this was done on the return trip to Fort Lincoln or during General Custer's interrogation of Rain-in-the-face is unclear, or if a beating or slap occurred at all. General Custer was able to obtain a confession from Rain-in-the-face for the murders of the two men.

Rain-in-the-face was detained in the guardhouse at Fort Lincoln after being convicted, as were a couple of grain thieves who General Custer had incarcerated. During Rain-in-the-face's wait to be hanged for his crimes, he escaped. Some think his escape was by design, to prevent an Indian uprising upon his execution. Two explanations have prevailed concerning the escape. One is that a hole was cut into the wall of the guardhouse by an accomplice of the grain thieves. The second story is that an elderly guard concerned with Rain-in-the-face's plight unlocked the handcuffs and freed him.

There may be credence to the theory that the escape was staged. Each escape plan involved the guards, either aiding the prisoners or in dereliction of duty (sawing a hole in the wall makes a lot of noise). With either explanation, the guards would have been severely punished, yet no record has been found concerning such a momentous breech of security in the escape of a noted war chief.

The repercussions of this arrest became legend during the battle of the Little Big Horn. It was reported that Rain-in-the-face caved in Captain Tom Custer's head, then cut out Tom's heart, took a bite out of it, and crushed it beneath the heel of his moccasin. After the battle, Rain-in-the-face fled to Canada with Sitting Bull, but later surrendered to military personnel upon his return to the United States. No legal procedures were brought against Rain-in-the-face for the murders of the doctor or sutler after his capture, even though he had been sentenced to death previously for the murders. Instead, he died a natural death many years later, thus giving more credence to the convenience of his escape.

Laundress Nash

Fort Lincoln had a laundress who later became well known through her death. Though married three times (with no divorce proceedings) making her a bigamist, she continued to use the name of her first husband, Nash. She was a tall woman of Mexican decent, who required a veil over the lower part of her face to conceal the facial hair she disliked so much. She was known for her abilities as a laundress, baker, seamstress, mid-wife, cook, penchant for frilly garments, and detail to feminine décor in her quarters. Her first husband, Nash, ran off with all the savings she had acquired from the numerous chores she performed throughout the post. Her second husband, a quartermaster's clerk by the name of Clifton, also ran off with a second cache of money she had saved. Her third husband, Corporal Noonan, did not repeat what the others had done to her previously, however the marriage ended in tragedy.

She openly told a few at the fort about her past, revealing that at one time due to hardships she had to dress as a man and had taken up the career as a bullwhacker (a person who drove oxen teams pulling wagons of freight). Though a rare occurrence, women were sometimes subjected to working as men or working along side of them to survive. Being out West without family to help during bad times, a woman had to perform work they normally wouldn't have done. Numerous women became "soiled doves" (prostitutes) exactly because of the lack of family support. Without previous skills, it was difficult for a woman to obtain employment, so they had to earn money, even if it was a degrading life. (Another woman who worked as a bullwhacker was Calamity Jane.) "Old Nash." as she was called, was much more feminine than Jane, but Jane chose to remain working the hard life. On the other hand, Old Nash chose to lose her male identity and became a laundress for the army.

While Corporal Noonan was out on campaign, his wife became ill. Knowing that she was about to die, she requested the women at Fort Lincoln not to go through any formalities with her death, and that she was to be placed in the ground without ceremony as soon as possible. Admired as she was, the women of the post took exception to saying goodbye to their favorite laundress with such informality. As they prepared Nash's body for burial, a secret was revealed. Mrs. Nash was in fact a man!

Upon returning to Fort Lincoln, with the well kept secret out, Corporal Noonan was taunted and ridiculed for his marriage to a man. The corporal insisted to the end that Mrs. Nash was indeed a woman, to no avail. Finally, Noonan could not stand the shame thrust upon him. He wandered into one of the stables and shot himself in the heart.

Comanche

Comanche was the horse of Captain Keogh, who was killed at the Little Big Horn. Comanche was a 6 year old light bay gelding standing 15 hands (five feet at the withers).

Captain Keogh, Brevet Lieutenant Colonel I Company, 7th Cavalry, bought Comanche for $90 near Fort Leavenworth, Kansas, in June, 1868. Captain Keogh soon discovered what Comanche was capable of in a pitched battle with a band of Comanche Indians at Bluff Creek, Kansas on September 13th, when Comanche was shot in the quarters with an arrow. The shaft had broken off during the melee with the arrowhead remaining in Comanche. Though wounded, Comanche continued carrying Captain Keogh throughout the battle undaunted. After the arrowhead had been removed, Captain Keogh named his valiant warhorse Comanche.

"Warhorse" is exactly what Comanche was, in every sense of the word. Not only was he wounded at the battle in 1868, but he was wounded in the leg fighting with the Comanches in 1870, wounded in the shoulder in 1871, and wounded in the right shoulder in 1873 during a fight with whiskey runners. Three years later, immediately after the battle of the Little Big Horn, Comanche was seen standing alone on top of Custer Hill with utter carnage around him. His saddle had slipped, hanging beneath his stomach, and his bit hung out of his mouth, but he stood vigilantly over the dead soldiers with 12 bullet and arrow wounds in his flanks, neck, and quarters. A reported rumor was that Captain Keogh was killed with a bullet to the head that passed through him and into

Comanche. After the battle the Indians reported Captain Keogh still held the reins of his faithful horse in his death grip.[21] A few decided Comanche should be put out of his misery, but Ferrier Gustav Korn, Captain Keogh's orderly, thought he could save him. Back at Fort Lincoln, his wounds were so debilitating he had to be supported in his stall by a sling. Ferrier Korn nursed him back to health and was his constant companion, until December 29, 1890, when Korn was killed at the battle of Wounded Knee.

That would not be the last history would hear of Comanche. In 1878, Comanche was involved in an unprecedented case. On April 10, 1878, the commanding officer of Fort Lincoln, Colonel Sturgis, issued General Order, 7, which mandated that Comanche was never to be ridden again by anyone, nor was he ever to be used for any work detail. Comanche, however was used for ceremonies where he would lead I Company. Comanche became basically a regimental pet. No place was off limits throughout the post, and that included flowerbeds or gardens. With his own special stall, Comanche became a very spoiled and pampered animal, and through this special attention, it is said, Comanche became particularly fond of beer. He had also been referred to as "The Second in Command: of the 7th Cavalry.[22]

But Comanche was not to be forgotten. On November 6, 1891, at the age of 29 Comanche died of colic at Fort Riley, Kansas. The decision was made to have a taxidermist prepare and mount Comanche and put him on display at the Columbian Exposition at the Chicago World's Fair in 1893. In 1902 Comanche was then displayed in the Museum of the University of Kansas in Lawrence.

Ninety-five years after the battle of the Little Big Horn, Comanche again claimed national attention by becoming the center of a controversial matter. It was deemed by

#193 Comanche with Ferrier Gustav Korn. *Courtesy Little Big Horn Battlefield.*

Indian students at the Kansas University that Comanche represented racial prejudice. In April, 1971, the Indian students considered Comanche a racial symbol due to the placard on the glass case he was displayed in, proclaiming Comanche as the only survivor of the battle at the Little Big Horn. Their argument was that there were Indians who survived the battle as well. They were correct, Comanche was not the lone survivor. He was not even the only surviving horse. There were many horses that survived, and the more able horses were led off for use by the Indians. Comanche was not taken because they knew he would have been little use to them and that he would more than likely die of his wounds. The students won their bid for the rewording of the plaque.[23] However, Comanche still remains on display at Kansas University.

It does not stop there either. Comanche has been the subject of several legal battles over the custody of Comanche's remains. Fort Riley has laid claim as well as Ft. Totten, Ft. Meade, Ft. Lincoln, and the Custer Battlefield National Monument Museum. General Wainwright, in 1947, sought to transfer Comanche to the U.S. Cavalry Museum at Fort Riley.

Comanche is one of the best known animals in U. S. history, and is probably the most litigated animal as well. In 1986, 110 years after the Battle of the Little Big Horn, Comanche again made national news when another custody battle erupted. This time it concerned water damage to Comanche from a flood.

The *Far West*

The *Far West* was a "stern wheeler" steamboat, sometimes called a paddle boat. By either name, this boat had a rotating paddle wheel located at the rear of the boat, as opposed to the sides, which propelled the boat through the water. Owned by the Coulsen Packet Company she was considered a mountain boat. This meant that her superstructure was smaller, therefore less weight and wind resistance. She had a 33-foot beam (width) and was 190 feet long. Unladen, she would only draft (the part of the ship that is underwater when floating) 20 inches, with 400 tons, a 4 1/2 foot draft. During the time period of Fort Abraham Lincoln, Captain Grant Marsh was in command of the *Far West*. Captain Marsh also had the distinction of navigating the Missouri River with Mark Twain aboard the *A. B. Chambers*.

The *Far West* was connected with Custer during two separate campaigns. The first was as the supply vessel for the Yellowstone Expedition in 1873 and the second was at the Little Big Horn Campaign when the *Far West* would be catapulted into infamy in 1876. She became the supply vessel and mobile headquarters for the Little Big Horn expedition. Over 200 tons of supplies were loaded on it and the boat supplied the expedition to the juncture of the Big Horn River and the Little Big Horn River. Once there, she acted as the forward base for Generals Gibbons, Terry and Custer, where they would plan their strategy to subdue the Indians considered hostile.

Fatefully, on the 29th of June 1876, the *Far West* became a hospital ship evacuating the wounded soldiers who fought at the Reno/Benteen battle site. Not having enough room for 52 wounded soldiers, Captain Marsh had excess cargo removed from the ship. This not only gave more room but it also lightened the boat giving it a much shallower draft for speed as

#194 Far West. *Courtesy Little Big Horn Battlefield.*

well as maneuvering over sand bars. Rumor/folklore has Captain Marsh ordering cases of gold being taken off and buried. However, upon his return trip upriver the gold could not be found due to a landslide covering the area where the gold was supposedly buried.

As preparations were being made to depart from the Little Big Horn area, it was reported they had one more wounded soldier to load. This last "soldier" became the most famous wounded passenger onboard. Comanche, Captain Keogh's mount, was loaded onto the deck, laying him down in hay by the stern wheel. Once Comanche was properly loaded, the *Far West* departed on the 30th June and arrived at Fort Lincoln on the 5th of July. In his rush to return the wounded soldiers to Fort Lincoln, the *Far West* set a speed record of 716 miles in 54 hours. This rate of speed, which averaged 13 miles per hour, included a stop to refuel for wood and two stops at other forts. This speed has never been equaled by another steam-powered boat down the Missouri. The *Far West* met its end on October 30, 1883, when it sank near St. Charles, Missouri after hitting a pile of submerged trees. On August 22, 1996 the United States Post Office released a 32 cent memorial postage stamp in honor of the Far West.

Tipi

A structure at Fort Lincoln not built by the soldiers but prominent around the fort was the tipi (Teepee, Thi' Pi). Tipi is actually two Lakota words, Thi', meaning "to dwell" and Pi, meaning "they dwell." The typical tipi was a practical design. With its geometrical shape to dispel the forces of the wind, it is aerodynamic and allows the wind to pass around it with the least amount of resistance. Conical in shape, the average size was 12 to 15 feet in diameter and about 12 feet high. Each tepee had approximately 10 to15 poles about 15 feet long and 1 .5 to 2 inches in diameter. It would take the women approximately one hour to erect or dismantle the tepee.

The functions of the tipi are more complicated than what we see. The walls were made from about 12 to 15 buffalo skins, which could be raised around the base in the summer to allow the air to flow through. For protection from the mosquitoes the Indians would place cedar greens around the tipi, which repelled the insects. During winter months a fire was used in a pit directly in the center of the floor. A flap at the top of the tipi was attached to an independent lodge pole that could be opened or closed to control the amount of draft for the fire's smoke to drift out.

#195 Tepee. *Author's collection.*

Deer skin was then used on the inside of the tipi walls. This served a triple function. First, the space between the two skins was stuffed with grass for insulation. Second, this air space between the skins helped to maintain the heat in the tipi by creating a dead air space. Third, the final aspect of this double skin was it created a draft, which helped pull the smoke from the fire out the opening in the top. The outside walls could be adorned with pictographs to display the warrior's personal accomplishments. The door was an oval opening with a very basic door made out of buffalo skin and wooden branches. It was more like a flap than what we perceive as a door.

McClellan Saddle

A piece of equipment invented prior to the Civil War and still in use almost 150 years later, with few alterations, is a McClelland saddle. Since 1859, this saddle was

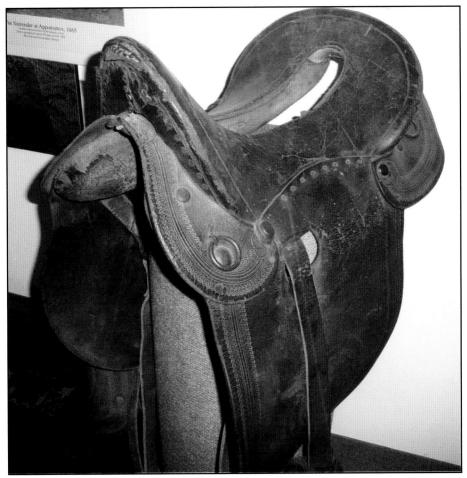

#196 Custer's McClellan saddle. *Author's collection. Courtesy Monroe County Museum.*

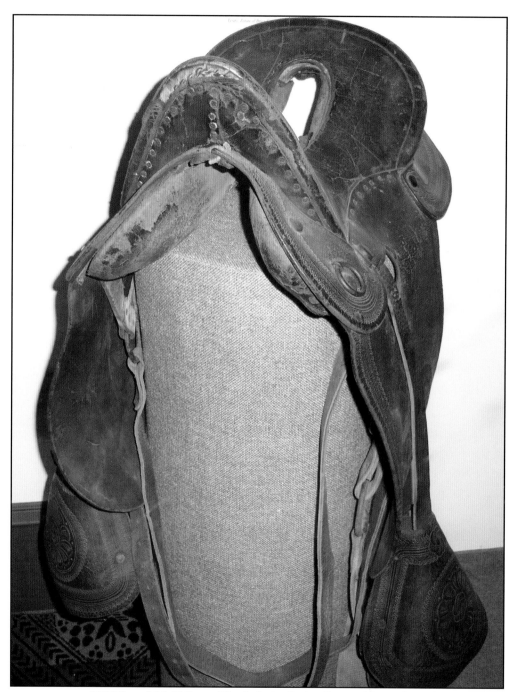

#197 Custer's McClellan saddle. *Author's collection. Courtesy Monroe County Museum.*

used by the 7th Cavalry as well as all U.S. Cavalry and is presently used by units of the military and police forces today.

Designed by George McClellan, former Commanding General of the Federal Armies during the Civil War and future presidential candidate in 1864, this saddle was a composite of several saddle styles. Manufacturing costs and the overall durability of the saddle were the major concerns being sought, but other factions of design came about due to prerequisites. It was inexpensive to produce, durable as well as light in weight, and a very basic design, thus making it easy to manufacture.[25] The unusual seat, called a "tree" gave it its distinction. Running the entire length of the seat was an opening about two inches wide. This saddle was not made for the comfort of the soldier but rather for the comfort of the horse. The lengthwise opening allowed the saddle to "breathe", preventing saddle sores and sweating. Also the opening allowed the saddle to spread out making it fit different size horses. An item that we see on most every other saddle is conspicuous by its absence. We have all watched westerns on television or in the movies where the most obvious part of the saddle is the pommel (saddle horn) sticking up predominately on the front of the saddle. This was an undesirable feature. Without it, the weight was reduced and it allowed the trooper to lean forward during battle.

Chapter 6
Fort Abraham Lincoln State Park

Campground

#198 River scene at campground. *Author's collection.*

I f you plan on camping at Fort Lincoln State Park, be ready to experience one of the nicest campgrounds in the United States. The staff at the park does a wonderful job maintaining the grounds as well as maintaining the serenity and peacefulness and integrity of the park that is nestled at the confluence of the Missouri and Heart Rivers. The campground has 95 sites, both modern and primitive. It has 30 amp electrical hook ups, water hook ups, dump station, host site, firewood sales, 2 camping cabins, a triple picnic shelter (each having its own fireplace), playground, amphitheatre, fire pits, walking trails, gazebo, volleyball court, reservation capabilities, and above all else, peace and quiet. For a special treat, listen as the sound of taps wafts its way down from the fort at dusk, bidding you good night.

#199 Campsite. *Author's collection.*

Fort Information:
Fort Abraham Lincoln
4480 Fort Lincoln Road
Mandan, North Dakota 58854
701-667-6340
800-807-4723 for camping reservations, an independent scheduling firm
Website: www.realnd.com/flmuseum.htm

#200 Little Miss Heather enjoying the campground with her father, Dan Stastny.
Author's collection.

#201 Campgrounds. *Author's collection.*

#202 Dan Schelske, Fort Lincoln Park Manager. *Author's collection.*

Fort Abraham Lincoln State Park has such a diversified menu of amenities beginning with the park itself. It contains a Visitor's Center/Museum, historic Infantry Post buildings, historic Cavalry Post buildings, interpretive tours, hiking and biking trails, picnic shelters, privately owned trolley rides, privately owned horseback rides, concession stand and campground. With 1,006 acres to patrol, Park Manager Dan Schelske and his staff do an excellent job making sure everyone who visits the park has a pleasurable and relaxing experience.

Interested in a personal guided tour of the Infantry Post? If so, be sure to sign up at the Visitor's Center. Enjoy an educational experience as Fort Historian; Jeff Hoffer walks you around the entire Infantry Post. Feel free to ask any questions, since Jeff is

#203 Jeff Hoffer, Fort Lincoln State Park Historian/interpreter, serving military duty overseas in Iraq. *Courtesy Jeff Hoffer.*

probably the most knowledgeable person concerning the history of the post. Jeff is also a 2nd Lieutenant with the Army National Guard. We owe Jeff a great deal of gratitude not only for his concerns for the history of Fort Lincoln but also because he recently returned from serving an extended tour of duty in Iraq. Thanks for being there Jeff!

#204 Visitor's Center/Museum. *Author's collection.*

Visitor's Center

The Visitor's Center is built of stone with a design that blends easily into the surrounding scenery. It contains a small museum displaying local artifacts and history. While there, an interpretive tour of the Infantry Post or the On-slant Indian Village can be scheduled. The tour to the Indian Village involves walking across a beautiful wooden bridge. As you enter the village compound, it is readily understandable just how well the village was protected from attack with the river to the east, the chasm over which the bridge spans to the south, and the palisade built to the northeast. Walk along as your guide explains the history of the village and enjoy entering the reconstructed Mandan Mound Lodges.

A side trip offered nearby is located downhill from the Visitor's Center. It is a 9 mile round trip trolley car ride along the Heart River. If you should become hungry or thirsty, visit the concession stand upon your return to the Visitor's Center, where you can also enjoy the serenity of the area as you sit in the shade. If you brought along your lunch, there are picnic shelters located around the park.

Cavalry Post

South of the Infantry Post, almost a half mile away, is the Cavalry Post, often called "Cavalry Square," that contains five reconstructed buildings. A granary, stable, enlisted men's barracks with attached mess, commissary and of course the Commanding Officer's Quarters, called "Custer House." Entry into all the buildings is freely allowed, with the exception of Custer House, which must have an escorted tour. The Commissary has a meeting hall, mock-up of a 19th century storage area and a gift shop. At the gift shop a tour of Custer House can be arranged, where a re-enactor from the year 1875 will guide you through the house giving a brief history of the fort. Please feel free to stop into the Commissary Store and meet Lucy Dahner, the Commissary Manager affectionately known as, "The Sergeant", or Dan Kautzman, and of course let us not forget Daisy the fort mascot. Lucy or Dan will be more than happy to answer any questions you have about the fort, as Daisy lies nearby listening intently. They are a cornucopia of information.

There is another side trip available near the Cavalry Post that also involves riding. West of the Commissary you have the opportunity to take a guided tour of the entire fort on horseback. Experience moving about the fort like the soldiers did while enjoying the aromas from the prairie grass and feeling the wind gently blowing upon your face. If riding horses is not your idea of fun, then enjoy the hiking and biking trails throughout the park.

#205 Rick Chambers enjoying the trolley car ride and scenery. *Author's collection.*

Infantry Post

A trip up the hill via vehicle or by hiking is a must. It is the location of the original fort once called Fort Mc Keen. There are three reconstructed blockhouses there with one having a sentry walk on top. Upon entering and climbing the steep stairwell to the sentry walk, experience a wonderful view. This is the preferred spot of the entire fort to let your mind escape the modern world like you did as a child playing "make believe." Remember how you could turn clothespins into people and play for hours with them? Lean forward on the railing and realize just how quiet it is, and then drift back, wondering what it was like back then. Look down upon the Cavalry Post and watch your imaginary soldiers, who appear the size of ants, walking around doing their assignments only known to them. See all the buildings as they once were, and then let your quiet reverie be disturbed by the gentle jingling of the snaps and eyelets of the tracers and reins of an imaginary team of horses. Listen for the creaking of the boards of the wagon and the huffing of the horses as they struggle to haul the wagon load of water up the steep incline. Ponder and try to imagine what it was like...............

After climbing down from the sentry walk visit the cemetery where 41 souls were interred, or the breastworks site where the Gatling gun was positioned. Walk around the post and see the foundations of all the buildings that once stood there. View the prehistoric mound located inside the post parameters, built between the years 400 B.C. to 400 A.D.

PLEASE LEAVE HISTORY FOR EVERYONE TO ENJOY

Gathering or collecting any artifacts found at Fort Abraham Lincoln State Park is illegal. Please leave them as you found them, then contact park personnel so the items may be recovered properly.

#206 Rick Chambers pondering atop the block house, "What was it like?" *Author's collection.*

Chapter 7

Civil Conservation Corps

T he Civil Conservation Corps (CCC) was established by President Franklin Roosevelt on March 19, 1933, as a program for people facing unemployment during the Great Depression. Under the president's "New Deal," CCC members worked outdoors for six months at a time, performing various construction work needed by the government.

Operated by the U. S. Army, this program employed men for $30 a month compensation, while supervisors were paid $35 to $45 a month. They could re-enlist for six months at a time, for up to two years of service. The CCC constructed roads, buildings, state and national parks, telephone and power lines, logging and fire roads for fire prevention, bridges, archaeological excavations, and furniture, and they planted trees.

Disbanded in 1942, the CCC employed over three million people, costing the government over five billion dollars.

Fort Lincoln owes a great deal to the CCC. In 1934 the CCC constructed the block houses and palisade, placed the foundation corner stones of the buildings to mark their locations, constructed the Visitor's Center, and built the roads and picnic shelters for future generations to use and enjoy.

In 2007, a bronze statue was dedicated to the members of the CCC for their work at Fort Lincoln State Park. It is located outside the Visitor's Center.

Appendix
Fort Abraham Lincoln
Timeline, 1872 to 1894

This Timeline has been gleaned primarily from Arnold Goplen's *The Historical Significance of Ft. Lincoln State Park*, North Dakota Parks and Recreation Department, 1988, second printing. To aid the reader, it has been categorized into chronological order.

1872
April 6. Original authorization by Secretary of War Belknap given for Fort Mc Keen

May. Survey party fired upon as it was going to Camp Green

June 14. Fort Mc Keen established, Lt. Colonel Huston, Jr. with Company B and C of the 6th Infantry, consisting of about 130 men, constructs the initial buildings.

Fall. Rail crew confronted by 120 Indians demanding food. The food was denied them so the Indians took it.

Fall. 3 mail carriers killed and scalped enroute to Fort Rice.

Fall. Indians attack killing the officer's cows.

November 19. Fort Mc Keen is renamed Fort Abraham Lincoln.

1873
February 11. Fort Lincoln Reservation declared by order of President Grant.

February. The 7th Cavalry is reassigned from the Department of the South to the Department of Dakota with Fort Lincoln being designated the Headquarters of the Middle District.

March 3. Authorization for the Cavalry Post at Fort Lincoln is given by Congressional Act.

Spring. Construction begins on the Cavalry Post by General George Dandy with the 7th and 11th Infantry consisting of 150 to 200 men.

May & June. 3 attacks by Indians on fort.

June 6-10. Twenty troopers commanded by Lieutenant DeRudio escorting a railroad engineering party back to the fort from surveying the Heart River, are attacked by 100 Indians and have a running battle back to the fort. Several Indians are killed but no troopers are harmed.

August. On the Yellowstone Expedition, Rain-in-the-Face kills the Sutler Balirand and Doctor Honsinger

September 21. The 7th arrives from the Yellowstone Expedition where Custer takes command of Fort Lincoln. With two companies going to Fort Rice, the remaining seven companies stay along with the 6th and 7th Infantry.

Fall. Command of the infantry changes to General Carlin.

1874

February 6. Custer House burns down.

Spring. Rebuild Custer House

April 23. A raid by Sioux Indians steal 90 mules from the parade ground. Custer leads the chase with 3 companies to try and recapture the mules. Company M is ordered from Fort Rice to help protect Fort Lincoln until Custer returns. Custer is able to recapture the mules but the Indians all escape.

May. Custer leaves to prevent a foray against the Arikaras and Mandans.

May. A battle is fought between the Arikaras Scouts and a War Party of Sioux within the Fort Lincoln Reserve as the inhabitants of the Cavalry Post watches nearby.

May. Major Reno leads a survey crew on the Northern boundary with Canada. This involves one company of troopers and the 6th Infantry.

July 2. Custer leads the Black Hills Expedition with 10 companies of the 7th Cavalry, one company of the 20th Infantry and one company of the 17th Infantry. With over 1,200 men this expedition had engineers, topographers, miners, botanists, photographers, journalists, paleontologists, zoologists, astronomists and newsmen.

December 11. Tom Custer takes 100 men to the Standing Rock Agency to arrest Rain-in-the-Face. The arrest is made on December 14th.

1875

April 18. Rain-in-the-Face escapes.

Unknown. Captain Marsh of the paddle wheeler Josephine takes Major Forsyth onboard to explore the Yellowstone River for possible future forts.

Unknown. General Terry orders civilian trespassers in the Black Hills to be kept out by Custer.

September. Secretary of War Belknap visits Fort Lincoln. He is snubbed by Custer due to Belknap ordering all soldiers to purchase needed personal goods through the sutler's store only.

December 6. The Interior Department orders all Indians to report to reservations on or before January 31, 1876.

1876

Unknown. Pickets and out guards attacked by Indians

February 7. Secretary of the Interior and General Sherman ordered to commence operations against hostile Indians.

March. Custer leaves for Washington D. C. to testify about corruption concerning the military post sutler system. Custer's testimony involved his disdain for Secretary of War Belknap and President Grant's son, Orville.

May. Custer returns from testifying in Washington. His visit was longer than expected due to his arrest and orders to remain in Washington.

May 17. The 7th Cavalry and 1 company of infantry leave for the Little Big Horn.

July 6. The Far West arrives at Fort Lincoln with the wounded from the Little Big Horn battle.

October/November. Colonel Sturgis with the 7th and 3 companies of infantry and artillery go to the Standing Rock and Cheyenne Agency to disarm and dismount Indians.

November 23. Lieutenant Gurley and the 6th Infantry go to Fort Stevenson to repair mounds (the guide markers for mail carriers).

1877

May. Colonel Sturgis leaves for the Yellowstone Area for the campaign against the Nez Perces.

October 21. Captain Baker with the 6th Infantry escorts a wagon train to Fort Buford.

December 31. The 7th escorts the Nez Perce prisoners to Bismarck.

1878

July. Ten companies of 7th scout the Bear Butte area to clear it of Indians.

Unknown. Telegraph lines are built between Fort Stevenson, Fort Buford, Fort Keogh and Deadwood, Dakota Territory.

1879

Unknown. Major Merrill with 3 companies of 7th Cavalry and Company B of the Infantry protect railroad crews.

November 10. Company B of the 6th Infantry establishes a cantonment (temporary quarters) in the Badlands for the protection of the railroad crews.

Unknown. Telegraph line established from Fort Lincoln to Fort Yates to Fort Sully.

1880

June 16. Company L of the 7th Cavalry intercepts hostile Indians from Lower Brule who were planning raids on the Berthold Agency

July 15. Captain Sangor takes the 17th Infantry to Bismarck to control riots by the striking steamboat men.

November 30. Company D of the 11th Infantry returns from protecting railroad crews.

December 3. Lieutenant English takes 12 troopers and Company F of the infantry to relieve the previous troops at the Cantonment in the Badlands sent in November 1879.

1881

April 13. Lieutenant English returns from the Cantonment with 12 troopers and Company F sent in December 1880.

June 26. Lieutenant Chance, Company G of the 17th Infantry goes to Bismarck to protect property at the quartermaster storehouse (distribution site for supplies to the forts in the area).

July 6. Lieutenant Chance and Company G of the 17th Infantry returns from Bismarck.

July 8. Captain Williams and Company F of the 7th Infantry goes to Bismarck to assist in the protection of the quartermaster storehouse.

1882

June. Troop L of the 7th Cavalry goes to the Little Missouri to protect railroad crews.

June. Headquarters of the Central Division on the Department of the Dakota is moved from Fort Lincoln to Fort Meade. Cavalry troops are no longer permanently stationed at Fort Lincoln.

Sometime between 1882 and 1883. The buildings at the infantry post are all dismantled.

1885

Unknown. 1885 to 1890 only 2 companies of infantry are posted at Fort Lincoln.

1886 to March 1891

Political battles rage to keep Fort Lincoln active.

1889

November. Ordinance Depot transferred to Fort Snelling, St. Paul, Minnesota.

1890

Fall. Two troops of cavalry and two troops of infantry from other forts arrive at Fort Lincoln to handle trouble at Standing Rock Reservation (Wounded Knee).

December. Troops leave Fort Lincoln to patrol the Cannon Ball River (December 28, Wounded Knee Battle).

1891

May. Orders to abandon Fort Lincoln

July 22. All troops leave Fort Lincoln

October 15. Fort Lincoln and Sibley Island are transferred to the Interior Department. Major Gooding is left in charge to guard the property.

1894

February. Major Gooding reports trees being cut and taken from Fort Lincoln Reservation.

December 1. 100 men raze the fort, tearing down almost all the buildings. Only 3 buildings left standing. Those caught and arrested were convicted, serving only 30 days in jail.

End Notes

[1] *The Soldiers*, David Nevid, 1973.

[2] *Ibid*

[3] *Ibid*

[4] *The Cavalry Battle hat Saved the Union*, Paul Walker, 2002.

[5] *Ten Years with Custer*, Sandy Barnard, 2001.

[6] *Unknown Civil War Soldier.*

[7] *Ten Years with Custer*, Sandy Barnard, 2001.

[8] *Boot and Saddles*, Elizabeth Custer, 1961.

[9] *Ten Years with Custer*, Sandy Barnard, 2001.

[10] *Ibid*

[11] *Custer's 7th Cavalry*, E. Lisle Reedstrom, 1992

[12] *Regulations for Uniforms and Equipment, G Company 7th United States Cavalry*, Phillip Owens, 2000.

[13] *Unknown Civil War General.*

[14] *Unknown 14th Century Poet.*

[15] *Unknown Civil War Soldier.*

[16] *The Historical Significance of Fort Abraham Lincoln*, Arnold Goplen, 1946.

[17] *Ten Years with Custer*, Sandy Barnard, 2001.

[18] *The Soldiers*, David Nevid, 1973.

[19] *Ten Years with Custer*, Sandy Barnard, 2001.

[20] *Ibid*

[21] *Speaking about Custer*, Sandy Barnard, 2001.

[22] *Ibid*

[23] *Ibid*

Bibliography

Barnard, Sandy, *Custer's Top Sergeant John Ryan*, Terre Haute, Indiana: AST Press, 1996.

Barnard, Sandy, *Digging into Custer's Last Stand*, Terre Haute, Indiana: AST Press, 2003.

Barnard, Sandy, *Speaking about Custer*, Terre Haute, Indiana: AST Press, 1991.

Barnard, Sandy, *Ten Years with Custer*, Terre Haute, Indiana: AST Press, 2001.

Brininstool, E, *Troopers with Custer*, Stackpole Press, 1994.

Capps, Benjamin, *The Indians*, NY, New York, Time-Life: 1973.

Capps, Benjamin, *The Great Chiefs*, NY, New York, Time-Life: 1975.

Connell, Evan, *Son of the Morning Star*, Northpointe Press: 1984.

Custer, Elizabeth, *Boots and Saddles*, University of Oklahoma Press: 1961.

Custer, Elizabeth, *Following the Guidon*, Bison Books: 1994.

Custer, General George, *My Life on the Plains*, University of Oklahoma Press: 1962.

Fougera, Katherine Gibson, *With Custer's Cavalry*, University of Nebraska Press: 1988.

Frazer, Robert, *Forts of the West*, University of Oklahoma Press: 1965.

Goplen, Arnold, *The Historical Significance of Fort Abraham Lincoln*, Bismarck, North Dakota, North Dakota Parks and Recreation Department: 1946.

Gray, John S. *Custer's Last Campaign*, University of Nebraska Press: 1961.

Miller, David Humphries, *Custer's Fall, the Indian Side of the Story*, University of Nebraska Press: 1957.

Moeller, Bill and Jan, *Custer a Photographic Biography*, Missoula, Montana, Mountain Press Publishing Company: 2003.

Nevid, David, *The Soldiers*, NY, New York, Time-Life: 1973.

Reedstrom, E Lisle, *Custer's 7th Cavalry*, NY, New York, Sterling Publishing Company: 1992.

Skler, Larry, *To Hell with Honor*, University of Oklahoma Press: 2003.

Urwin, Gregory J. *The U.S. Cavalry*, Blanford Press: 1984.

Utley, Robert M. *Cavalier in Buckskins*, University of Oklahoma Press: 1988.

Walker, Paul D. *The Cavalry Battle That Saved the Union*, Gretna, Louisiana, Pelican Publishing Company: 2002.

Websites

www.mcpheetersantiquemilitaria.com. Antique military items.

www.nps.gov.libi. Little Big Horn Park

www.realnd.com/flmuseum.htm. Fort Abraham Lincoln

www.gov/is/hist. State Historical Society of North Dakota

www.aaamunitions.com. Ordnance

www.nps.gov/archive/foda/fort_davis_web_page/home.html. Fort Davis

www.ast press.com. Author Sandy Barnard

www.us7thcavcof.com/gcompany.html. Uniforms

www.ushistory.com. Uniforms
www.theflagguys.com. Flags
www.corbins.com. Bullets
www.trapdoorcollector.com. 1873 Springfield Rifle
www.trapdoors.com. 1873 Springfield Rifle
www.gatlingguns.net. Gatling guns
www.wikipedia.com. General information
www.gramlichservices.com. Web site construction
www.navyarms.com. Weapons
www.usa1hp.com.webpages.charter.net/net/usa1hp/armyhome.html. Insignia
www.7thuscav.homestead.com. Bugle calls
www.usmilitaryhistoryinstitute.com
www.stevensclaroff.com. Photography
www.shebbyleetours.com.